Living the Colors

Living the Colors

V. Hanumantharao

Allied Publishers Pvt. Ltd.
NEW DELHI • MUMBAI • KOLKATA
CHENNAI • BANGALORE • HYDERABAD

ALLIED PUBLISHERS PRIVATE LIMITED

1/13-14 Asaf Ali Road, **New Delhi**–110002
Ph.: 011-23239001 • E-mail: delhi.books@alliedpublishers.com

17 Chittaranjan Avenue, **Kolkata**–700072
Ph.: 033-22129618 • E-mail: cal.books@alliedpublishers.com

15 J.N. Heredia Marg, Ballard Estate, **Mumbai**–400001
Ph.: 022-42126969 • E-mail: mumbai.books@alliedpublishers.com

No. 25/10 Commander-in-Chief Road, Ethiraj Lane (Next to Post Office) Egmore, **Chennai**–600008
Ph.: 044-28223938 • E-mail: chennai.books@alliedpublishers.com

P.B No. 9932, No. 15, 3rd Floor (Next to Vijaya Bank), 5th Cross, Gandhinagar, Karnataka, **Bangalore**–560009
Ph.: 080-41530285 / 22386239
• E-mail: bngl.journals@alliedpublishers.com / apsabng@airtelmail.in

Sri Jayalakshmi Nilayam, No. 3-4-510, 3rd Floor (Above More Super Market) Barkatpura, **Hyderabad**–500027
Ph.: 040-27551811, 040-27551812 • E-mail: hyd.books@alliedpublishers.com

Website: www.alliedpublishers.com

ISBN: 978-93-90951-07-9

Published by Sunil Sachdev and printed by Ravi Sachdev at Allied Publishers Pvt. Ltd.
1/13-14 Asaf Ali Road, New Delhi - 110002

Acknowledgements

My sincere thanks to Allied Publishers, New Delhi for publishing the book.

I am grateful to Mr. Jagdish Singh for all his efforts in bringing out this novel in a nice shape.

1

Ashok, began getting rid of his poverty-stricken unpleasant childhood years, by first erasing memories of past connections. He avoided persons of those days as he progressed well in life.

Ashok, a postgraduate in engineering in his late twenties, tall and with a pleasant disposition had a way of impressing people well.

He succeeded in establishing and developing a factory, making component parts for Defence departments.

One day he was in office, discussing with the suppliers during the course of his business dealings.

He unexpectedly encountered an unwelcome person who came to discuss with him about his tender. He was one of those three shortlisted suppliers. But Ashok was unaware of his antecedents.

The stranger as he entered, was aghast at seeing Ashok his childhood friend and forgetting propriety, he shouted aloud, "Shake! You here?"

Ashok was stunned finding that childhood acquaintance in front of him. He would not call him a friend now.

He, however recognised him as 'Green', who used to wear green shirts or pants always, in those days. He was well dressed and looked urbane now. As for the term 'Shake' Ashok was nicknamed so for his poor knowledge of English language, that being the short of Shakespeare.

Ashok made a grimace and regained his composure at once and waved the other to a seat in front of him. He looked in to the papers once and politely asked him to wait for the reply in a week.

And as to Green, he realized his mistake at once and assumed the posture of a person who needs favours from the other.

Ashok's P.A., a young man in his early twenties, who was standing beside him and who was a witness to this unpleasant encounter was non-plussed and kept his normal demeanour. Ashok looked at him and satisfied with his facial expression which showed no trace of amusement.

Later, when he was in bathroom, Ashok recalled the incident of 'Green' and his facial expression, when he brushed him aside for his misbehaviour, while showing him a seat. That brought him a broad smile. He thought for a while, whether he could have been more polite and especially as the other person was on a business visit. Nevertheless, the present incident against the incidents of his humiliation at the hands of 'Green', in those days brought him satisfaction, for a short while. The feeling of revenge was not deep rooted in his mind.

* * *

He used to be the butt of jokes by his classmates, in his young age. Two reasons stand out clearly even by today's analysis. One was, his father's poverty which reflected in his and his mother's travails. The second was his physical or personal deficiencies. Certain incidents of those days stand green in his memory and tease him again and again. Might be that he was a sensitive person by nature. But if such incidents repeatedly happen any one would become sensitive as the pain was such.

One evening, he was at the stationery shop, situated next to the main gate, in school premises. His mother sent him there as he needed note books urgently. He asked for two notebooks of two hundred pages, one each for himself and his sister Bala. The shop was crowded as usual. The shopkeeper gave the books to him and stretched his arm for money. Ashok, then pulled out four ten-rupee notes from his pocket and gave him. The shop keeper asked ten rupees more. Ashok searched in his pocket and there were none. He remembered to have one more ten-rupee note in his pocket. What happened? Did he lose it on the way? Or he was mistaken of that extra note. The shop keeper was in a hurry and he at once returned the money and took back the books. Ashok heard someone laughing loudly. It was his friend 'Green' and he felt ashamed there in front of others. Moreover, his class mate Lalitha too was there. When he looked at her, she too was smiling might not be for hurting him, but it was an added injury to him. He ran back home empty handed. He was ten years old then. That incident, he could not erase from his young mind for many years. Even now it hurts him badly. That fellow 'Green' remained a bad guy from those days. Young Ashok told his mother of that incident. But she could not redeem his image as she had no more money on hand. She pulled him close and pressed to her bosom. He remembered the feelings on the face of his sister standing nearby.

That apart, another incident of his young days churns his heart. During Dussehra and Pongal festival days, they fly kites in the evenings. Children of the neighbourhood were playing with kites during the Pongal festival at the playground near their houses. His sister and her friend 'E' were flying the kites by themselves. They were in long skirts with matching blouses and upper cloth. His friend of those days D and himself—they were in tenth class—were flying kites along with other friends and neighbours. Sister's friend let the thread slip long suddenly. And the kite flew out of control and got stuck in a branch of the neem tree in one corner of that playground. Ashok ran after that and tried to take hold it. He could not do that. The branch of the tree was at a higher level. He tried to reach for it by jumping up a few times but could not succeed. In the meantime, 'D' came over there and picked up the kite just by standing on his toes. He was taller to him then. They were in pants then, aged around ten plus five. He earned the smile of gratitude of the girls. He then patted Ashok on the back as if to console him. It was very humiliating. He was singled out for his shortness in front of the girls. Of course, later on, in degree class he grew up very tall to six feet. One of his friends commented that he looked like a hero in English movies. Anyway, that bad incident left a scar on his delicate young mind. 'D' became a bad guy for him thence forth.

* * *

Two more incidents come to his memory when he thinks of his native village, Koduru or dear parents.

Because of poverty, there were problems for having new dresses. The number of pants and shirts for him used to be very limited; four sets in all. Compared to others this must be very meagre because he used to come across others; 'Green' or 'D' used to change dresses every two days. He used to wonder how could anybody afford so many sets of clothes. As for him he used to get the old clothes of his father sized up to his measurements to have a new pant or shirt. So, his friends used to make fun of him with the comment, "you are in new clothes". In fact, they were sized ones and they knew that, because, they used to suppress their laughter with those comments. 'Green' and 'D' were very prominent in making such comments and hurting him.

At least for sister, who was two years younger to him, his mother used to insist on, for really new ones with the comment that 'she is a girl'. Another reason was that sister could not have sized clothes of mother because she wore skirts not *sarees*. His father used to consider her case as special because of these reasons. His mother Parvathi, used to go by the decision of his father always.

Another worse case of humiliation was when he failed in ninth standard. There would not have been much publicity for this. But because his maternal cousin who was younger to him by a year became a class mate to him now as he repeated the ninth class with his cousin. That humiliation lasted for one full year. Luckily, his maternal uncle got a transfer in his office in the subsequent year to another place. As long as they were in the same place, his aunt used to highlight this, to all relatives whomsoever she met. So, that cousin of him became an avoidable acquaintance for him. He used to avoid meeting him wherever possible.

But his father never discouraged Ashok and used to say that even some great scientists failed in their examinations. He didn't know if that was true or his dad used to say so, to please him.

But, because of his general ability and hardwork he overcame all those drawbacks of early life later and outsmarted his classmates of those years. Now, none of those guys could stand a chance alongside him in money or name.

* * *

His father, Mr. Krishnarao worked as a high school teacher at his native town, Koduru. He used to be in *dhoti* and shirt as many teachers used to wear in those days. He was a good teacher in mathematics. Many students used to come to their house for tuitions. Their parents used to come with their wards and stand outside their house to meet his father. It was said in those days that his father used to charge very small amount of fees. He used to think that his dad felt bad, in taking money for teaching at home. But it became necessary for him as the expenses were high and the salary, he used to get from school was not sufficient. Some girl students too were there. He remembered the face of 'J', a beautiful girl. She was in tenth class.

Now, his father and mother still lived in the old house of their grandfather. His dad did not make a house. He could not afford to. All his savings were finished by the time he married off Bala, his daughter. In fact, their education had eaten away much of the money earned by his father. His parents even now lived there happily contented. They did not want to come to the city to stay with him. They liked the town life at Koduru and their erstwhile contacts more. Yet, sometimes they visit him. His father insists on staying at the native place only. Ashok never forced them to come to him. He provided whatever they wanted and needed there only, like air-conditioners, washing machine and a car. But his father sent back the car with the driver, stating that he did not want the pomp in that small town. His sister Bala, now lives at Mumbai with her husband Venkat, an engineer in a company there. They had a five-year old son, Jaggu.

As Ashok was not accepting her proposals for his marriage, his mother asked him to marry a girl, he liked. He managed to postpone all her pleas for visiting the girl's houses, to select the bride. She brought forth some alliances from relatives too, but he rejected them all on some pretext or other. Now, she got vexed and stopped raising that topic with him anymore.

* * *

2

Ashok came down the stairs to the portico in his bungalow at Maharani pet, Vizag. It was his habit to look either side of the portico, to view the ambience of the beautiful foliage and exotic trees amongst the native ones, extending beyond to the high compound wall.

It took quite a few minutes for the car to tread on the well-laid pathways for reaching the main gate. The guard paid respects while closing the gates. Ashok earlier instructed them, opening the gates was more important than saluting him.

The car moved along the broad roads to the comparative narrow roads to reach the highway.

After a while, Ashok looked up from his laptop towards the driver, when the car screeched to a halt suddenly.

"Sir, someone came across suddenly." He added "He is a school boy on a bicycle."

The driver, at once opened the door and got down.

There were not many on the road then. The school boy dusted off his half pants and dashed off in to a by-lane in no time.

At a distance, inside the roadside tea-stall, two persons who were sipping tea got up to rush towards the road after keeping the tea cups on a make-shift table. They retreated after seeing the boy disappearing in to the by-lane.

With a sigh of relief, the driver opened the door and took his seat.

"No injuries sir, only some scratches on his right arm."

Ashok said "O.K.".

Ashok remembered the day when he too got involved in an accident long back—he was ten years old then-at his native place, Kodur. He was riding fast on a bicycle with Kishan at the back. When they turned suddenly on to the main road, Dr. Z's car, which was going slowly hit them. Both he and Kishan fell down. There too was a tea-stall on the other side of the road. A number of people were drinking tea and some munching snacks. In small towns, it's a past time for people, to go to a tea-stall and have tea whenever they find time. A few of them rushed towards the road. They did not allow the car to move and they abused the driver for his negligence. The driver tried to defend himself saying the boys came on the road suddenly. However, the drinkers of tea did not accept that and one of them held the collar of the driver. Then Dr. Z had to come out of car. He paid some money and appealed to them to release the driver.

At a distance, a police constable standing near the cross roads was found to be walking towards them. The gathered visitors from tea-stall took the money and left the place at once. And the car of Dr. Z zoomed away in no time.

Ashok and his friend laughed off the incident and returned home.

Ashok did not want to remember the names of those guys of childhood days either really or due to indifference for them.

Another incident of his childhood days—he might be ten plus four years old. They used to live in a joint family. In addition to his family, two uncles and one aunt, all younger to his father and their families too used to live together in the grandfather's house. The grandparents were active and used to attend to their work by themselves. They were not dependent on younger generation for any of their daily chores and needs.

He was looking out the window from his room, of course not entirely his, that's boys' study room. He was looking at the girls, his sister and her friends. They were talking loudly, while walking around the front-garden which was full with flower pots of plants of varied colours and types. The front-garden though not large, was good enough for one to take a stroll freely and enjoy the ambience. If that was so, the house of grandfather was not big and was made in a standard plot of a couple of hundred yards or around that size. The housing board makes plots of that size only to cater to the middleclass people.

But as children, they never felt in those days that it was not enough for their playing or other activities. Now when he looks back, he could make out that in younger days, the feelings were more important than the sizes of houses. In youth's perception the utility has more value and consideration than sizes or their values. No kid would feel that his father was not rich enough to provide for, his requirements. Of course, many parents luckily fulfil most of the requirements of their children. That house of grandfather had whatever other houses around, had for the dwellers. So, his grandfather's house had flower shrubs and plants and a spring-well providing for drinking water. It had all the requirements of the inmates and they never needed to go out for anything other than groceries and medicines.

Now, returning to the present story. Ashok was looking out the window at the girls. Nobody was around to watch his antiques. He knew, he was alone and watching the girls talking and playing in the front-garden. Their giggling and moving hands up and down appeared fascinating and attracting for the teenaged boy's mind. When he ponders over that now, he gets transported to an exciting experience, what might be called romantic feelings.

Suddenly he heard "Hi, Ashok, you mischievous boy! Here you are!"

That was his aunt who breezed in, without any sound or warning. Of course, he missed her silk *saree*'s 'swish' sound, which comes in swift movement. Obviously, she saw him watching the girls. She laughed aloud and gone as quickly as she entered the room, after picking something from the almirah. Any way, he was distracted and could not enjoy the scene any more. He ran out to his neighbour K's house. Krishna was the name.

Now, when he thinks over those incidents and feelings, he considers the present-day movies would pale away before those incidents of angelic romance. The movie could move an adult mind to the heights of sensuous feelings but not comparable to a teenage sense of imagination and sweet perception.

Now, Ashok was watching a movie scene in a song sequence and could no more enjoy that after getting back to those days of his life suddenly.

He now turned the channel to a news bulletin and next to that of a discourse by a monk of some order. The monk exhorted the viewers to inculcate ways of improving one's life by learning from past life and incidents. Life consists of various incidents of the past and when you look at the conglomeration in a proper perspective, you will be able to observe the beautiful clear image of purity. Never judge any incident to be unattractive or bad, but consider the totality of the blessings.

He said if you look back at life at a later stage, the incidents look beautiful as colours, as if you look down from a mountain, the plains appear smooth and attractive, all the rough stones and verdant grass fields spreading together.

Live life like a butterfly, gather good things and leave bad, but learn lessons on the journey, the monk said.

* * *

Ashok did not marry till now. When he comes across a beautiful maiden, appearing someone like 'Y' or 'J' of those days, he feels an urge and thinks why not get married and lead a happy life. But will it be a happy life? The question arose. He remembered the story, his friend Mohan's life story, narrated by him a few months back.

Mohan a smart young man of his own age, loved his classmate Ramya, a beautiful and wealthy girl. He married the girl of his choice. They liked each other and they were in college then. Luckily, girl's family had distant relationship with the family of Mohan. They also belong to an ancestry of rich culture and wealth. So, his parents did not object. And the girl's family too agreed without much persuasion, as Mohan too belonged to a wealthy business family. Girl's mother had a longing to give her in marriage to her brother 'P's son who was an industrialist and had good political connections. But as the girl persisted on, her mother had to yield to her choice. They were married at last with the ready consent of her sensible father, Mr. Maruthirao. The marriage was performed at a hill station a few summers before. They invited only close relatives on either side to avoid unpleasant incidents with those whose matches were ignored. The bride's side arranged flight tickets for the small group of invitees. They booked many hotel rooms for the stay of all of them comfortably. The marriage was performed in a cool and comfortable environment. The couple flew to a predetermined foreign location for their honeymoon.

Life went on well for them for a few years. Mohan's mother, Annapurna, yearned for a grandchild and urged his son and daughter-in-law Ramya, to have a child before long. But Mohan's mother-in-law had other views. She wanted her only daughter to head the industry-to take the reins of Dad's estates—as they planned before. Sour feelings persisted in both families for some time. But Mohan and Ramya did not mind that and led a happy time.

Mohan's mother became sick suddenly while on tour to U.S.A. on a visit to her daughter's family. After returning from abroad, she felt that she must see a grandchild, so she might not regret the unfulfillment of her desire later.

Mohan pleaded with his wife to have just one baby and then she could concentrate on her father's business. Ramya felt she must concede to the desire of husband's family on this issue. She persisted in convincing her mother to accept the just desire of the in-laws.

At last, Ramya's mother Mrs. Lakshmi, consented to the pleas of her daughter, on the condition that the new born child must be taken care of by the parents of Mohan. Her reason was that, then Ramya could handle the business affairs of her father as required, without hindrance. The issue was that Ramya's father goes abroad frequently, on business for long periods, and hence he needs someone to take care of business matters with responsibility. At last, the matter was resolved as Mohan's mother happily agreed to take care of her grandchild.

However, they could not fulfil the desire of Mohan's mother. Ramya could not conceive even after many months. The doctors said Ramya would not be able to conceive a child at all. They tried with many fertility treatment experts, but of no avail. Same medical opinion was given by all medical consultants.

Ramya felt humiliated in the first few days. Mohan consoled her and told that no one could predict the future and hope was essence of life. She reconciled to the happenings at last. After that, she began concentrating on her father's business. In the course of busy schedules of work, she forgot the unpleasant issue.

Mohan's mother became sick again, this time for a longer duration. Mohan was disappointed for not being able to fulfil his mother's desire. His father felt it as a stigma on the family, though personally, he was not an orthodox person.

Ashok had been recollecting his friend's painful story.

At this point of time, Ashok got interruption to his chain of thoughts. He had an intercom message, a business connection was on an urgent call.

Once, the call was finished, Ashok stopped thinking about Mohan's personal affairs.

He began analysing the write up about a new project, which was suggested and proposed by Dr. Varada his consultant, a Research Associate. In fact, Dr. Varada was a class mate to him in post-graduation. Dr. Varada works for a multinational firm dealing with multiple products used for defence equipment. He likes to dress well and appears in suit in all formal gatherings. Certain ideas when he developed exclusively for use by Mr. Ashok's firm, Maxima Productions, he passes on the details in a report. They discuss about the possible production setup available and then Ashok prepares the viability report.

Incidentally, Dr. Varada was introduced to him by Mohan. Though he knew him as a classmate, he was not knowing Dr. Varada as a Research Associate before that.

* * *

One morning, Mohan called Ashok and asked him if he could spend some time with him at the New Wave Hotel that evening for some urgent personal discussion. Ashok was taking his breakfast. He agreed readily. He could make out that the matter was important, as Mohan's voice was grave, unusually so.

Ashok met him at the hotel. In that exclusive meeting, Mohan discussed about the estranged relationship between his wife and himself. He said his wife had talked of divorce. It appeared his mother-in-law encouraged her. Ramya was set to increase her participation in Dad's business. After talking about the personal misunderstandings between them, Mohan withdrew in to silence with a sad expression. Ashok too could not speak for some time. And after thinking for a few moments, he advised him to try to procrastinate the issue as long as possible. By that lapse of time, she may understand the implication of divorce and the damage that causes to her reputation.

That much he knew about Mohan's marriage and his subsequent troubles. Ashok did not hear from him further. Ashok hoped and concluded that they were reconciled and settled in life.

But all these episodes of Mohan's marriage and difficulties of later life, strengthened Ashok's adverse views about marriage. And so, he decided to keep away from thoughts of marriage.

* * *

Mr. Rajesh was a practicing accountant, who advises Ashok, in accounting matters. Rajesh had a side business of real estate, managed by his brother Sunder, a class mate of Ashok. That connection made it possible for him to get the work of Ashok. Sunder was independent and straight forward and never sought any help from his friend. That only brought him closure to his friend. Ashok waited for a long time before he took Sunder in to confidence. Ashok wanted a reliable accounting adviser and asked Sunder about that. And Sunder knew that Ashok would not allow childhood contacts in his present life. However, with the changed relationship, Sunder suggested Rajesh's name. Ashok accepted him, as he needed a reliable person for accounting matters.

* * *

3

The City Club had many facilities as required by the club goers anywhere. In the words of non-clubgoers, a club was supposed to be a place where wealthy idle guys spend time playing cards with high stakes. Of course, the founders always take care not to entertain people from lower strata to join the club. The reason was to avoid lowering the status of the founders of the club and also the members. Now, people who intend to become members of the club too check the status and standing of the founders as also the members there.

If this was one aspect, there was the case of aspirant persons, who would like to have a place to spend evenings and weekly holidays, playing outdoor games like tennis and shuttle badminton and so on. Those who could not strain themselves on outdoor games, and do not like gambling—the card games were called so—spend time playing carroms or chess. But according to the norms of such a club, the aspirant members must be of elite and rich background or socially respected professionals. They also include senior officials in government. To keep the ramp high, club fees would be prohibitive for ordinary middle-class persons.

A club is a place where one makes friends and this helps many in need to further their careers in business or other vocations. There would always be occasions to come together in games or functions of the club. The affinity in clubs leads the members to mingle in personal celebrations too. Of course, individual members may be selective in choosing others, for games or functions.

Now, Ashok met Mohan at the tennis court here. When Mohan made scorching volleys which the opponent could not play back, Ashok clapped wholeheartedly. Mohan was special in that technic and Ashok had many occasions to appreciate Mohan.

Mohan had opportunities to hail Ashok, when he served the ball. Many a time there were few opponents who could return the service of Ashok in that club's tennis teams.

In a rare gesture, Ashok accepted Mohan as a close friend. In course of time, Ashok came to realize that Mohan was a sincere and good friend. They used to meet at the functions of the club to start with. Later they met on many occasions, whenever there were functions in their respective business seminars or meetings at the state or All India level.

Mohan's family had a large timber business established at R' Mundry. Mohan's father Mr. Dasaradh belonged to Rajolu, at an hour's drive from Rajahmundry. His forefathers lived there only and developed business at Rajahmundry. Mr. Dasaradh stayed near his farms in his ancestral bungalow. His brother Mr. Narender, lived in his own building at a short distance to his brother. Mohan's sister Vani was married and stayed with her husband Sankar in U.S.A.

Mohan had developed medical equipment's business, after obtaining dealership license of an All India Brand. He keeps himself busy with business matters and visits the club whenever he was free. He would not involve himself in the business matters of his wife, Ramya. She managed the business of her father by herself, whenever his father was away or whatever work was allotted to her, if he was home.

Mohan never enquired about Ashok's disinterest in his marriage. And Ashok would not meddle in the personal matters of Mohan, unless he was asked for his opinion.

* * *

4

Rajesh, the accounting consultant of Ashok, had a friend Omkar. Omkar was connected with his real estate business, which was looked after by Rajesh's brother Sunder. Omkar one day visited Rajesh in his office with prior appointment.

He said "Rajesh, my friend, I am in need of your support for my real estate agency. You are well established as an accounting consultant. Your real estate business can take care of itself. Your brother, Sunder is a good man but he would not shift even an inch from his principles. Sometimes we need to change the prices and values according to our competitors and market. Please put in a word to your brother, about my troubles. Please ask him to ignore my dealings if they are not normal, sometimes. Please help me."

Just then the phone rang, Rajesh said "Yes, Mr. Ashok, I will be there by nine, tomorrow morning as you wanted. Tomorrow, morning I am free. I will bring the details of Maxima Productions taxation. O.K. yes, I can spend a few hours with you there."

He kept the phone down.

Omkar "Who was that Ashok? Is he, that boy from Koduru. He was in my class."

Rajesh "Yes, he is a friend of my brother Sunder. I am now his consultant."

Omkar smiled "My brother is now a B.Com. graduate. Please recommend him to Ashok. He can fix him in his company."

Rajesh "You don't know, Ashok now. He does not want any contacts of Koduru near him. He is antagonistic to you people who made fun of him in those days."

Omkar "Those were childhood days. He should not grudge that now. Any way please try for me."

Rajesh "O.K., I will try. But I know him and also the result in advance."

* * *

Mr. Rajesh, came to meet Ashok as per the appointment, for resolving some accounting matters. They discussed at length for two hours about the accounts and taxation matters of his company Maxima Productions. Ashok cut off all other calls and work of lesser importance.

They were served coffee and snacks as and when required.

They discussed and made extensive notes for over two hours.

Maxima productions in course of time faced more competition. Supply to Government agencies always depends on the relationship with the individual officers influencing the purchases. So, when the setup changes, the priorities change. Maxima mainly depending on one customer group for offtake, had to suffer vacillating demands and hence production shortages or excesses.

Ultimate analysis was, it was not in good shape.

Rajesh too conveyed that opinion to Ashok. He agreed with Ashok in diversification of the products. He said either he must work out vigorously to get more orders from the government companies or diversify in to other areas.

In respect of taxation too, when the customers were private parties, the supplier was forced to show less turnover by falsification, as the customer does not want the real and higher figures. This is not workable in the business with Government. So, it affects garnering profits.

Ashok said he was in touch with his technical consultant Dr. Varada, to explore the ways to diversify in to a different kind of products, which was more profitable and independent of the present setup of customers. He said he wanted to go for public utility products which could be sold through dealers.

When Rajesh got up to go, Ashok asked him about his brother Sunder, who was in real estate business. Sunder was a classmate of Ashok.

Rajesh with solemn voice said "Sir, my brother's son is in hospital due to some chronic problem. Both my brother and his wife are running back and forth to hospital and home."

Ashok expressed his concern to him and asked for the name of the hospital where Sunder's son was admitted.

After departure of Rajesh, Ashok called Sunder on phone. He enquired about his son and told him that he was coming over there to see his son.

Ashok, after half hour, called his driver and proceeded to Quick Recovery Hospital where Sunder's son was admitted.

Sunder and his wife were in the general ward, where his son Sreedhar, was being treated.

They both stood up after seeing Ashok.

The Duty Doctor came and checked up the patient's B.P. and other parameters. He glanced through the patient-record sheet.

Ashok asked him the progress. The doctor said as per the diagnostics reports, he was suffering with respiratory infection and it might take a week or more to recover.

Ashok told Sunder to shift the patient to a special room.

Sunder said "Mr. Ashok, it's O.K. We will manage here. It would be expensive. The amount payable for the whole process could be burdensome."

Ashok said "My friend, don't bother about the amount. Come on, we will go to the payment counter and finish the formality. We will shift him to special room. He will get better attention there and it is necessary."

Reluctantly, Sunder accompanied Ashok and they went to the payment counter and Ashok paid all the expenses for pending bills and also for shifting Sreedhar to a special room at once.

Ashok left them only after the patient was shifted and made comfortable.

Sunder and his wife expressed thanks to Ashok with tearful eyes for his affection towards the friend's family.

Ashok, after reaching his office, called the office of Quick Recovery Hospital and after introducing himself told them that he would clear all the bills of the patient Sreedhar, Mr. Sunder's son. So, he urged them to take care of him well.

* * *

5

Mohan called his wife Ramya and told her that he wanted to meet and talk to her. Ramya was busy with a conference of Dealers of North-India states. Ramya looked after the business of her father and spent most of her time in that.

She said "Will be free by evening. We can talk then. Please come to my dad's place."

"O.K. but we will meet at my residence. Or if you don't wish to come there, I will come to your guest house."

She accepted. "O.K. I will be there by six o'clock."

Mohan was in office. It was lunch time. After a while, his mother called.

"My dear, how are you? Is Ramya there now?"

"She is not home yet. Right now, she is busy in office with business matters."

They eat lunch together at home.

He did not pass on the information about the divorce issue to his parents.

His mother continued "Alright, Dad wants to talk to you. He is fine. Just casual talk."

His Dad "Mohan. How are things? Ramya has not come home yet? Some misunderstanding?"

"No. Dad. We are talking on phone. She is busy with her Dad's business matters."

"O.K." His Dad switched off phone.

* * *

Evening when Mohan went to the guest house, Ramya was in the hall of the guest house, sipping coffee. After seeing him, she ordered one more cup for him.

They sat down to talk.

Mohan started "Ramya, I had been thinking of the matter all these days. I felt it is not necessary to go for divorce now. I think we can wait. More-over, I am not after children."

She said, "That's not the point. If there is no other possible solution, as this situation, it is better to go our ways. No problem."

"There is no hurry. You please think over. Consider its impact on your reputation, as also mine."

"No, but Ashok it's about your mother's aspiration; I don't want to keep her disappointed. And I don't feel personally anything about separation too. Why not settle down well with peace of mind."

Mohan "Please consider postponing it for a few months. And, in future whenever you feel like, we can meet. That is up to you, Ramya."

Ramya smiled "O.K., can we go then? Mom and I are to go to a relative's place."

He too smiled and said "Fine."

* * *

6

The local Good Health Hospital was not big but there was provision for round the clock service for ten inpatients. Many outpatients visit day time. No specialist doctors were on rolls, but if required they arranged specialists.

Ashok's father was admitted there for breathlessness the evening before. He had mild asthma attack.

Ashok reached Koduru by eight in the morning, a couple of hours after he was informed of the incident. Koduru was of a couple of hours drive from Vizag.

He sat beside the bed of his father. That was a general ward. There were no special rooms in that hospital.

"Yesterday, in the evening he ate a banana. I was doubting. Your dad is allergic to banana fruit, you know that. But he did not heed. His old student brought a dozen Chakrakeli variety of bananas from his village. He likes Chakrakeli very much, you know and could not resist the temptation. He ate one only and sneezing began within minutes and then cough. We waited till eight o'clock. The trouble did not cease. Then I called Subbu and told him."

That was his mother, Parvathi's narrative of the incident.

His father now intervened "I said no to hospitalization. But Subbu insisted saying if it aggravates in the night it will be difficult."

"So, he called an auto and we came over here. Subbu was really helpful as always."

His mother continued.

Subbu was Ashok's paternal uncle Mr. Narasimharao's son who resides on the next street with his parents. He had a motor bike and goes around on that.

Just then Subbu came there.

He said "Hi, Ashok. Uncle is fine now. I spoke to duty doctor. He said after a while, by ten o'clock, we can take him home."

Ashok got up from his chair and shook hands and patted him on the back. Subbu was younger to him by two years. He was employed in the revenue department locally.

As Subbu had to go to office, he left them after a while.

When the regular doctor came and checked the patient, Ashok was permitted to take his father home.

Ashok called his driver and they went home in his car. Ashok bought the prescribed medicines on the way.

His mother cooked food for them. He had to leave after lunch only, as his mother insisted.

While passing through the town, Ashok came across only one known person Chandra sitting on a bench at the cigarette kiosk at the end of the street where his house was.

Chandra looked at the passing car curiously, as it was new and big compared to local cars seen on the roads. Ashok avoided eye contact and did not know if Chandra looked inside.

The Welcome Hotel, the first building on the adjacent street was busy with customers. He used to go there sometimes, when his mom sent him in the morning for bringing a parcel of *idlis*. Very rarely he sat inside as it was a costly fare. That happened only when his uncle came from abroad. He used to take Ashok with him. They would eat *puries* and bring parcels for parents and aunty and sister. The breakfast there tasted good. He could not visit the hotel now, even though he could afford that. That was the irony, he could not afford when he was there and now when he could, he would not visit because of the status. Either way he could not enjoy the tasty and lip-smacking snacks there. Ashok heaved a sigh of disappointment.

When they reached the end of the main road that entered the highway, the Gandhi park was standing as a benchmark of permanence. Any other building would not last that long as with the price rice, old buildings would tend to be demolished and new ones rise as they fetch higher rents.

* * *

Chandra folded the newspaper he was reading and looked again at the car. He could see the backside of the head of the insider. He must be Ashok, he guessed. From the side window, he saw him, rich and elite looking. That big car and all that glitter made out that he was a rich man from city. He had already heard about Ashok, the ruffled half-pants guy of old days. He was junior to him in the high school.

Now, Chandra called the shop fellow "Hey, Subhash, you saw that car. That was Ashok going in that big car alone. Maths teacher Krishnarao sir's son."

"Is it? I have not seen. I am busy with the betel leaves rolling for this Kittappa fellow. Why is he going away already? I heard his father was not well yesterday."

"Yes, that is so. In fact, in those days, I wished to go to Krishnarao sir for maths tuition. But my father was not interested in my studies. My father said I must stop studies at ninth class. He was afraid if I pass tenth class I would insist on going for intermediate and then degree class. He wanted to keep me beside him in shop. My uncle was already asking for my marriage with his daughter 'Mumu' studying in seventh class."

Subhash laughing loudly "Yes, yes. I know. Your father is a shrewd man. Anyway he knew that you would not pass tenth in one go."

Chandra got angry and threw the newspaper on the bench and rose up to go.

Subhash to cool his temper "O.K. O.K. you are right. Your dad wanted the fat dowry from your uncle."

Chandra took the betel roll from Subhash and left.

* * *

Ashok walked in to the long dining hall of sixty feet by thirty feet. It takes care of a few dozens of guests at a time.

He sat on a chair close to the kitchen.

He called the head chef "Nair, can you get me a cup of your good coffee."

Nair said with a smile "Yes sir, at once."

"Nair, where is your junior chef?"

He refers the assistant so.

"Sir, he went to the vegetable market."

Ashok asked him. "You did not send him to the super bazaar this time?"

"No, sir, 'Vel' is afraid to go there."

He was smiling.

"Why?"

"Sir, Vel is not accustomed to the big markets. He gets confused with the display of so many items and their variety. He said he gets tempted and puts one or two nice things in his pocket in spite of him. I think he was caught twice. Once he paid the amount and came out. Second time, I had to go there and got him released by telling that he worked in your bungalow."

Ashok burst out laughing.

"My God. You dragged my name in this."

Nair too laughed, yet, he thanked his stars as boss did not take it seriously.

* * *

7

Three months after Ashok met Mohan on the latter's divorce issue, Mohan called Ashok and asked him if he would join him to go to Rajolu, his native place to celebrate Deepavali, the festival of lights. Ashok said he would find out his appointments and let him know the position.

Ashok spoke to his P.A. and found that because of the festival, there were not many engagements. Only two dealers of Chennai wanted to discuss some matters, but that could be postponed for two days. Deepavali was not that popular as Pongal festival in the deep South.

So, he agreed to the proposal, little knowing that Mohan was going with his wife, now reconciled with him.

After knowing that, he said he would come in his car and stay there a few hours and then proceed to his native place to spend the festival with his parents.

* * *

Mohan's ancestral house at Rajolu was in an acre of land adjacent to the lake Nallacheruvu, meaning black lake. But the lake was full and overflowing with crystal clear water. Many a time, names do not denote the true picture of the person or thing.

The house, in fact, a bungalow was a large building, extending to over a ten thousand square feet in area with two floors. The structure was made of lime mortar and black stones. On both sides of the bungalow, a total of hundred acres of fertile land was there inherited from their forefathers.

They reached the place in their cars by six in the evening. The three of them strode up the broad steps to reach the large hall in the ground floor extending to a thousand square feet. It had furniture and fittings made of old teak wood. The door way, they entered had doors engraved with intricate and pleasing designs and made of high-quality teak wood. Even though they were made about a hundred years back they do not appear to need any renovation or maintenance. When Ashok looked up, he saw the roof, very high might be eighteen feet high.

Mohan asked Ashok to occupy one of the large sofas, while he sat opposite him in another one. Ramya went inside the house saying she would meet her in-laws.

Mohan laughed aloud after passing his glances up at the high roof and said "Ashok, you see the roof—it is so high—old standards to keep the inmates cool in summers."

Ashok too laughed and said "You don't need air conditioning here."

Mohan "My family is in timber business since three generations. So, all furniture and fittings in this building are made of teak wood. They don't need any maintenance. The polished wood lasts for generations."

"We feel very comfortable here. The cool breeze from the lake is also an added advantage."

"Yes, yes, the door at the back allows gusts of cool currents in. We feel relaxed oncc we are in the hall."

Now, Ramya walked in accompanied by her in-laws.

Mohan and Ashok got up and greetings finished, they all occupied seats.

Servant boy brought tea and snacks for them.

While taking tea, Mohan's father Mr. Dasaradh asked Ashok "Mr. Ashok, you are from Koduru. Is that your ancestral place?"

"Yes, sir, we belong to Koduru only. My father Krishnarao garu worked as a teacher in the high school there. My parents live there only even now."

"I heard about Krishnarao sir, maths teacher of Koduru. He is well known all over the district."

Mr. Dasaradh said with a broad smile.

Ramya and her mother-in-law were engrossed in their chit chat.

After a while Mohan said "Dad, Ashok wants to go back to his place after a while to be with his parents."

Mr. Dasaradh said "I understand. His parents expect him. We cannot force him to stay here."

He smiled benignly.

Mohan said "I will take Ashok upstairs and show him the lake and surroundings."

"O.K. Fine."

Mohan led his friend to the broad stairs at the centre of the hall. The stairs about eight feet in width, took three turns to reach the top, and had three landings one at each turning.

The stairs led to a hall and then the wide terrace with immediate entrance to a long corridor covered with asbestos sheets.

Once they came over to the open-to-the sky balcony, they felt the heavy and cool breeze of Nallacheruvu on the southern side.

Ashok looked around the balcony and saw large areas of green fields on two sides of the building and a black topped road on the north side.

They strolled around the balcony chatting for some time and then Ashok wanted to go back to his place, as the sun was receding in to the west and darkness was enveloping around.

They returned to the ground floor.

Ashok took leave of the parents of Mohan and Ramya and walked to the portico accompanied by Mohan.

Ashok reached home before it was dark. It was an hour's drive from Rajolu to Koduru.

* * *

Deepavali day—Ashok was at his home town with parents. His mother applied oil on his head which was supposed to be blessing on younger people. Both dad and mom sprinkled turmeric touched rice on his head as a good omen for future, as they were doing to him in his childhood days. He did not object as he felt that was an opportunity for them to be very personal with him. His mom said she was missing her grandson, son of her daughter. Her daughter Bala, son Jaggu and Venkat, the son-in-law were at Mumbai. Ashok felt he replaced Jaggu, son of his sister, on that occasion. After that he went for bath with shower. That procedure was followed in many households still unless they were very modernised.

After bath, he changed in to new clothes, a shirt and *dhoti*, already kept ready by his mother.

Then prayer to God in the *pooja* room along with mom and dad.

At this point Subbu came in. Having come to know that Ashok was there, he came in the morning. Otherwise, he used to come in the evening of festival days, to be with Ashok's parents.

Ashok's mom readied breakfast of *idli* and *upma* for all of them in the dining hall.

Ashok had good time with Subbu for some time and then Subbu asked him to accompany to his home on next street. Ashok preferred going in car as he did not want to meet any old acquaintances even by accident. However, he did not say so to Subbu. He just told him that he preferred going in car as it was available readily. Subbu agreed. Ashok met his uncle and aunt and Subbu's daughter Neelu there. Ashok gave a gift of five hundred rupees to Neelu, in spite of objection by Subbu and his wife. Ashok left them in half hour as his mother insisted that he should be back at once. After all, he was not visiting them on every festival day. In fact, he visited them because he was there to Mohan's place on his wish to accompany him, though he was busy with office work.

Ashok left them, the next morning early by eight as he had an appointment with a business connection.

* * *

8

Mohan did not give a chance to displease Ramya and was as before with her. She knew his mother was not happy with him for not insisting on the issue of grandchild.

Ramya though busy with her dad's business, she kept the issue of getting a child in her mind all through.

She met one day her friend Suguna, a doctor, her childhood friend and classmate.

When the topic of children came up, she, being a gynaecologist, told Ramya, "Nowadays it is not necessary to lose hope about that issue as there are umpteen ways of getting a child." Ramya insisted she did not want to adopt a child as it would neither be satisfying to their family nor to the family of the child who was given in adoption. At this point of discussion, Dr. Suguna suggested surrogacy as the best method for her to go for. Ramya said she would talk to her husband and then call her back.

One evening, she raised the topic with Mohan. Mohan felt very happy that Ramya was still thinking of his mother and her wish. He said whatever method that was not harmful to her health and possible was O.K. for him. They discussed the ways and means to go about that they have to consider alternative ways and wanted to discuss with doctor further.

* * *

Ramya called her doctor friend and asked her for an appointment. On that day she and Mohan went and met her in her clinic.

Doctor Suguna "Do you have someone in mind for this purpose? You must have enquired and made up your mind."

Ramya "Yes. I have considered some of my contacts suitable for this purpose as told by you. One Mrs. Jaya who works with one of our offices has agreed."

"Has she children and what's her age?"

"She has two children and she is thirty-three years old."

"Fine, how about her husband? Will he accept this?"

"He does not mind and he would not go against her wish. Moreover, her parents are very loyal to my family and my dad helped them in many ways. She was settled in life by my dad only."

"That's O.K. We will check her health and suitability."

"Whenever you want, I will bring her here for that purpose."

Mohan heard the conversation.

He said "O.K., doctor, thank you for your help."

Dr. Suguna told Ramya that she will call her after two days.

* * *

As per the appointment, Ramya and Mohan reached Dr. Suguna's clinic and Jaya was with them.

Dr. Suguna called them in. Ramya and Jaya went in, while Mohan waited outside.

Dr. Suguna asked Jaya to go in with her, for conducting tests.

After half hour, they returned. The doctor said that she will prescribe some more tests for Jaya and they were to be done at the designated labs of the fertility centre to which hospital she was attached.

After getting the reports, she said the procedure would be started.

* * *

A week later Ramya and Mohan went to the doctor with the reports. The doctor checked the reports and she gave the schedule of procedure for the surrogacy operation. She told them that the procedure would start after a week.

After a week, Jaya was admitted in the fertility centre of the hospital.

* * *

9

Dr. Varada wanted to meet Ashok about the new project. That was a month back, he gave him the broad details of the proposal.

He called and asked Ashok whether he studied the report. Ashok said he had some idea of the project now and would be glad to discuss with him the details. He was free to meet Dr. Varada that evening.

* * *

Ashok wanted to expand his business in to another line of activity. Dr. Varada suggested production of special wood panels which could replace non-load bearing walls in construction work. Much research work was done and extensive trial applications were conducted. Some pilot projects were done by some noted construction companies for low cost housing for weaker sections. The reports were satisfactory. The project report contained all such details.

Dr. Varada asked Ashok "Mr. Ashok, is the outline given in the report is sufficient to have an idea?"

"Yes. I have gone through the report and it shows it has potential to be in business for a decade at least. That appears O.K. About investment I have to think over alternatives. I will discuss with some known sources and find a solution. How about market? It is a new product and requires much introductory work and advertisement. Have you any information on that?"

"I am trying for some sources who have contacts in this business. I will check with them."

"O.K. Dr. Varada, we will meet again after ascertaining these details."

"Alright. Mr. Ashok."

After departure of Dr. Varada, Ashok called Mr. Mohan.

"Hi, Mohan. Dr. Varada suggested a new business proposal. I was planning to expand in to some new line. That is to keep myself sufficiently busy to overcome the marriage proposals from my contacts and family circles. This appears to be one way out."

Mohan laughed out loudly "Is that so? Not furthering business ambition?"

Ashok too laughed and said "Any way, both can go together. Coming to the proposal, it's a project requiring more investment than what I can afford to. So, I considered calling you."

"That is quite O.K. What is the line of business?"

"That is a new product. It is making of special reinforced wood panels which would replace non-load bearing walls in construction work. It is revolutionary."

"But there were reports of such a wood in the news some time back."

"No. But this wood takes care of entire walls in a building where load bearing is not priority."

"Now I understand. It appears to have good potential commercially. But a lot of initial work is involved for convincing people to go for it. Much advertising is necessary. But how about competition?"

Ashok "I agree. This is new to society and market. But it has huge potential. As of now competition is very little. Mohan, if you are O.K. with new business, we talk this over when you are free."

Mohan agreed in principle.

* * *

After a month, Dr. Varada called Ashok and told him that he succeeded in getting a headway to reach a source for marketing the special wood. He said to start with, it was a construction company of high standards and rich background and reliability. But they wanted a guaranteed supply and confirmation by a reliable source for financial viability of long-term supply. At present they are planning to switch over to housing for middle class people at affordable cost, of course not low cost.

Ashok said he would certainly give a positive reply shortly and asked him to keep that source intact.

Ashok knew Mohan's father Mr. Dasaradh could fill in, the reliable source for guarantee as his social and financial standing was good.

Later, Ashok called Mohan and asked him to give some time for a discussion with him and that was regarding the new and interesting project, about which he already told.

Mohan called Ashok after some time and told him that he would be glad to meet him on the approaching Sunday. Ashok okayed it.

Mohan continued and said he would be happy to host him at his house at Rajolu.

Ashok agreed and said that would be ideal for undisturbed discussions.

* * *

On Sunday morning, Mohan reached Ashok's place and picked him up. The plan was to spend time till evening at Rajolu.

The driver took them on a smooth drive while they enjoyed chatting about village life and how it was good to lecture on political platforms or discuss in elitist seminars about the preference of village life over city life. But no youngster would like to leave the city for a village life.

After a couple of hours journey, they reached Rajolu. Ashok was welcomed by Mohan's father, who was reading newspaper in the hall of the bungalow.

Dasaradh took the coffee cup back in to his hand, while the servant boy brought two more cups of, flavour spreading fresh coffee for the friends.

It was nine in the morning.

After coffee, Mohan excused himself and told his dad that they wanted to go upstairs to discuss about a new project, enjoying the cool ambience of the terrace.

His father laughed and said "Wish good progress in discussion."

Ashok and Mohan reached the flight of steps to reach upstairs.

In the open terrace, they had a table and two chairs readied for a comfortable discussion.

Ashok passed on the project report to Mohan. While he was glancing through that, they discussed the business details.

Ashok "Mohan, this is a big project needing an investment of one hundred crores rupees. The report says so and it included working capital. Of course, some financial agency would come forward to offer a loan of seventy percent on guarantee."

Mohan "You said something about market?"

Ashok "Yes, Dr. Varada. In his latest call to me said that a construction company wanted a reliable source of supply. It appears they need continuous supply of wood products once they start a project. But they want assurance of supply from a guaranteed source."

Mohan "But that does not take care of entire production. We have to conduct some seminars and convince the elite society. If some news about the acceptability appears in media, then there will be good demand."

Ashok "I know. This will be a starting point only. We must get a demand for continuous offtake, of the produce. That means we must get dealers too, who keep stocks. Of course, that happens only after what all you have said was done. I agree a lot of initial work is involved. But it is challenging and has good commercial potential."

Mohan "O.K. it is interesting. Challenge part I like."

He smiled.

Ashok "The cost includes payment of royalty to patent holder, a research institute of government origin."

Mohan "No problem, government institute means reliability is assured."

Ashok "Regarding investment we must be prepared for thirty percent. As far as I am concerned, I can come up to fifteen percent."

Mohan "No problem, I will take care of the rest and any shortfall too."

He smiled and patted on the palms of Ashok who kept his palms on the table in a relaxing mood. Ashok too smiled and took Mohan's hand in his as a gesture of comradery.

Ashok said "Thank you. I am glad you are prepared to join me in this."

He continued "I will talk to Dr. Varada and fix up with him for a discussion. Of course, after he comes forward about more users or dealers."

"Sure, I agree."

They switched to general discussion for some time. The servant boy came up to call for lunch. They folded the papers and made for the ground floor.

Already Mr. Dasaradh was waiting in the hall.

They walked over to the dining hall.

After a long and sumptuous lunch, they returned to the front hall.

Mr. Dasaradh enquired about the new project. He showed enthusiasm in the new product. He felt that kind of wood product would have good future market and he encouraged them to go right ahead.

After a while, he left for his usual afternoon siesta.

Mohan and Ashok had a conversation for some time about their businesses.

Mohan then said "Do you like a boat trip on the lake?"

Ashok laughed and said "Why not, I will be happy to see the nature at its real looks unlike in the movies."

They walked to the back of the house and then reached the well-laid footpath leading to the shore of the lake where two boats were floating in water as they were tied to a large tree there. Two boatmen ran forward seeing them.

Mohan called one of them and fixed for taking them around on the lake.

They walked on the wooden ramp and jumped on to the boat. The motor boat started at once and took them to the other end of the lake. Then it began making rounds around the lake in a slow movement so that they could enjoy the trip. Ashok took snaps of the nature around full of greenery and tree branches moving in the cool breeze. The beautiful ambience aroused their spirits and Mohan began singing an old Telugu movie song aloud. Ashok laughed and joined him. The boatman was all smiles. He was happy to see the visitors in such a happy mood. The birds on the trees were watching them as they looked at them. The village urchins playing in the waters had hearty laughs. They were happy when the city guys became like their own folk.

When the sun began going down, they returned to the shore and Mohan paid the boatman well beyond his expectation.

Ashok looked in to his watch and said "Its time I started back."

They retraced to the bungalow.

After taking leave of Mr. Dasaradh and Mohan, Ashok was back on his return journey to the city. Mohan stayed back.

* * *

10

Ashok received an invitation card from Mohan for the marriage of his cousin.

That was for the marriage of Mr. Dasaradh's brother's daughter and it was a week days later at Rajolu.

That evening he received a call from Mohan extending a special invitation to him to attend the marriage. He asked Ashok to bring his parents too, to the function.

On the day of marriage, Ashok called his dad and asked him if they could accompany him to Rajolu for the marriage. His dad said as the marriage was in the night, they would not be able to come. Moreover, Mohan's family was not known to them before, it would not be proper to seek any special needs for them in the night, as they were old.

So, Ashok went alone to Rajolu, on that evening.

Mr. Dasaradh's brother Narender's house was in another part of Rajolu. It was a modern building constructed in a large area. The entire front portion of the house was covered with colourful tarpaulin cloth and was well lit with bright lights making the night dazzling.

Mohan received Ashok at the entrance of the hall.

The main hall in the first floor of the huge building was decorated for the marriage function. The hall in the ground floor was made ready for reception in sections designated for different kinds of refreshments, snacks and drinks.

As the marriage function was yet to start the invitees were received and led to the reception facility.

There was a round park next to the main gate. The vehicles enter from one side and could leave from the other. The park had cement benches in rows. Varied flower plants in bloom were all round the park in pleasing arrangement.

Mohan took Ashok around the park, while they were talking with each other.

At that moment, Mohan's cousin Sagar, brother of the bride Neelima came there. Mohan introduced him to Ashok.

After making a round, they entered the hall again. Each of them took a glassful from the drinks available there.

A young lady of twenty plus came there and smiled to Mohan and Ashok. She signalled Sagar closer and told him that he was wanted in the marriage hall. Sagar excused himself and left.

Mohan told Ashok "Ashok, this lady is Mala, sister of the bride and Mala, this is my friend Ashok."

Mala smiled a dazzle and folded her hands in a beautiful gesture with a bow.

Ashok too bowed to her. He could not shift his eyes from her.

Mala asked "Mohan, why Vani is not here?"

Vani was sister of Mohan.

"She could not come, as brother-in-law was busy with work."

Mala smiled and told Mohan "Brother, I have to go. There is some urgent work."

She again bowed to Ashok with a broad smile and left.

Ashok could not turn his gaze away from her direction for a few moments.

Mohan with a smile touched him on the shoulder and said "Mala is not married and they are looking for an eligible groom."

He indirectly suggested to him.

Ashok with a hint of red on his face asked him "Mohan, what is she doing now? I mean is she studying or in job?"

Mohan "She is a software professional and is now at Vizag."

Mohan led Ashok to the first floor for attending the function. He took him to his uncle Mr. Narender, bride's father and introduced him. Mr. Narender smiled and shook hands with him. He excused and left them as he was busy with the rituals of marriage.

Mohan accommodated Ashok in the first row in front of the dais, for a good view of the function. He then left him to receive guests arriving at the entrance to the hall.

There, Ashok had many occasions to watch Mala from a distance.

The function had not begun yet. Guests of either side, bride and groom were arriving in herds, many of them local people. During this period, Ashok wanted to go to rest room and left.

By the time he returned, his seat there was occupied by someone. He could find a seat in the third row beside two elderly looking men. He settled there at once.

Those two elderly men appeared to be close friends or relatives to each other. They were speaking to each other intimately.

"Venkayya, I sometimes feel very lonely after she left me to reach her heavenly abode."

The voice was very pathetic and he must have lost his wife a short while before, might be some months before.

The other person said in a sympathetic tone "Rangayya, it might take time to become normal for you. For old people of either sex, that is inevitable. One would leave the other first and the survivor had to suffer the agony. I heard on T.V. the other day a saintly man, telling that the remedy for this is to develop friendship with another person in close circle, might be a relative or friend of same sex. There should not be any misunderstanding in that. If that was cultivated even before such a calamity, it would be good he was telling."

"It is easy to talk like that but only the person who suffered the loss would know the pain."

He added "I think the best way to cut this short, is old people should not worry much for any ailment and must be prepared for the ultimate thing any time ever. This separation is also a kind of ailment, I think."

At this moment, the loud speakers began blaring out the utterances of the *pandits* performing the ceremony. Ashok did not hear any more conversations or they might have stopped talking then.

The marriage function began with all urgency and fanfare.

At the time of felicitation after the conclusion of the function, Mohan introduced Ashok to the newly married couple, Neelima and Shyam.

After dinner Ashok left for home.

* * *

11

Ashok with the help of Rajesh got all the permissions required for starting the new industry, including the pollution control department, as the industry produces effluents. Rajesh took necessary steps for approaching a nationalised bank for the loan. Mohan's father Mr. Dasaradh furnished the guarantees required by the bank.

They named the Partnership Firm as 'The Perfect Wood Products.'

They were allotted required land in the Government industrial estate, after payment of the scheduled fees. The building plan as per the rules was made and got approved.

The plan provided for the factory building, office and go-downs for raw materials and finished wood products.

Mohan and Ashok accompanied by Mr. Dasaradh, earlier made a few visits to the industrial estate before finalizing the site.

On the day of ground breaking ceremony, Mohan invited Mala as advised by his father. Mohan informed his father about Ashok's liking for Mala. He knew Ashok had a nice and favourable feeling towards Mala.

Ashok too was pleased to meet Mala once again. After the ceremony they had coffee and snacks in the temporary enclosure made of canvas cloth. The bank officials and industry department representatives were present. Rajesh was there too as he was the prime mover for the official work part.

After all the invitees left, Mr. Dasaradh told Mohan to arrange a family get together at a good hotel on the happy occasion of starting a new business.

When Mr. Dasaradh was not in the hearing range, Mohan told Ashok that he could have more familiarity with Mala and talk to her, and his father too liked Ashok and treats him as one of the family members. Ashok smiled and said he too wanted to talk to her, taking the opportunity of her presence there. Later, when she came there, he smiled and greeted her. He said they could meet sometimes being in the same city.

Mala asked Ashok "Can I meet you in your office, when I am free from work and it's boring?"

Ashok smiled "You are welcome any time. Just make a call."

He gave her his card.

Ashok later told Mohan that he had been thinking of meeting Mala, since he met her at her sister's marriage function. And he could get the opportunity now unexpectedly.

Mohan said "Ashok, now you can come out of that lonely life at last, as you liked some girl first time."

He added "As you know each other, it would be good for you, to go ahead further. I would be the first person to celebrate the culmination of mutual liking."

* * *

Ashok did not wait anymore, he called Mala after two days. After meeting Mala at the ground breaking ceremony, he felt he was missing something in life. He already lost some opportunities earlier, though appeared to be within reach. He now concluded that it was he who let them slip away. He also felt that Mala might not be his, if he tarried any further. He resolved that he must meet and propose to her whatever she might think. He did not want to lose her with his delay. He called her from his office,

"Hi, Mala, hope you are fine. Today I am free. Will it be O.K. for you if we meet today over coffee?"

"Hi, Ashok, yes, after four in the evening it is fine."

Ashok smiled "Then I will drive to your office and we will go to New Stars Hotel. We will have some good time there."

"O.K. that would be fine. When you reach here, you please call me."

"I will be there by five, o.k."

"Yeah. I will close work and be ready by that time."

That evening, Ashok picked up Mala and reached New Stars Hotel near the Beach.

They moved to Coffee Shop.

"Yes. Mala, how is office?"

He made a beginning.

"I am fine. I have been working there for two years. Nothing new about work. Moreover, my dad is one of the major shareholders in the company. But he would not use his influence for my advantage in office."

Coffee and snacks arrived by then.

Ashok "How do you spend the holidays here?"

"For small breaks, I have some friends and we go to Malls and Restaurants. The problem is with longer breaks."

"Why?"

She smiled. "Not a big one. My parents insist on my marriage whenever I go to my native place."

Ashok laughed "But why? What are your plans for future?"

Mala laughed "My parents are looking for 'some good matches' for me, in their words, that is, a person meeting their eligibility criterion."

She diverted the subject "How is the new project work going?"

"It is going with good progress. We ordered for the machinery. And main raw material wood is the subject of Mohan. Some other materials are available indigenously."

Ashok reverting to the marriage subject "What kind of matches are in your parent's 'imagination'?"

He asked with a smile.

She laughed "As far as I know they want the match from a known family and of a well settled person."

She continued with a smile "I understand you are not in favour of marrying."

"How do you know?"

"My brother Mohan told my parents."

Ashok laughed and said "That was some time back. Now, I want to marry if I come across a girl like you and if she agrees my 'match'."

He laughed for emphasizing the word 'match'.

"I am honoured and elated with your statement."

She laughed with apparent glint in her eyes.

He said again "Yes. I like a person like you. Why? I like you. I only want an answer."

"I am taken unawares. Of course, my brother Mohan used to tell about you. If my parents agree, I will be happy to give a positive answer."

She laughed with bent head in obvious modesty, natural to a girl.

They finished coffee.

Ashok said with a smile "I will convey this to Mohan with confidence now. Then, my parents would talk to yours."

Mala gave a smile in agreement.

Ashok dropped her at the Ladies Hostel.

* * *

After reaching home, Ashok called Mohan,

"Mohan, I am happy to announce a good news to you. I talked to Mala, we met at a restaurant and spoke with each other over coffee. She is favourable to my proposal. But she said she wants the consent of her parents.

Mohan cutting short Ashok "That's great news. You ventured well. I feel happy for that. I will do one thing right now. I will call my uncle, that is Mala's father and tell him to proceed further. So, give me a few moments to call to him."

Ashok laughed loudly "Thank you, Mohan. Go ahead."

He switched off the phone.

Mohan called his uncle and told him about the good news. Narender too was glad that Mala was agreeable to marriage now and the groom was none other than a friend of Mohan and known to him well.

Narender and his wife then talked to Mala for a long time and appreciated her decision.

He then spoke to Mohan and asked him to fix a date to meet Ashok's parents.

* * *

They fixed the visit to Ashok's parents on an auspicious day.

Mohan and Ashok reached the latter's modest house at Koduru that evening.

Ashok made the front room well-furnished and clean. Room freshener was in place.

Mr. Narender and his brother Mr. Dasaradh accompanied by their wives and Sagar, the former's son, arrived there.

After greetings, they settled in the small room as comfortable as it allowed them to be. The discomfort of the visitors was apparent, Ashok could sense.

Narender said as Mohan was a friend of Ashok, they could approach them with ease.

Ashok's father, Mr. Krishnarao expressed his happiness as Ashok at last agreed to marry.

He felt happy as the bride was from a neighbouring place.

Mr. Dasaradh said the name of Mr. Krishnarao was familiar as a noted mathematics teacher in the district.

After refreshments and all, Mr. Narender and his wife invited the groom and his parents to visit their house and see the girl. Mr. Krishnarao agreed and said Ashok would inform the date to Mohan.

* * *

Ashok after fixing up with Mala, visited her at her office. They met in the reception hall.

Mala's friend, Sarada, came there, to see and appreciate her friend's selection.

Mala introduced Ashok to her.

Sarada seeing Ashok smiled and said "Why, I knew him as my senior in the school. I am very glad for your selection, Mala."

Ashok saw her and at first taken aback seeing Sarada unexpectedly and at once collected himself and with a smile said" Yes, yes. I know her. She was in our school at Koduru."

They sat there for a while and Sarada excused herself and left them. The conversation between Ashok and Mala ranged from the funny things at her employer company to the visit of her parents to his place Koduru and all the other good things. Ashok asked her to call him when she was free in the evenings so that they could go to beach or some place to spend good time.

Mala asked him "Do you like to have coffee here?"

He smiled and said "Certainly."

She told the receptionist for coffee.

After coffee Ashok left.

* * *

Late in the night, Ashok began assessing, once more his resolve not to entertain memories of his painful childhood. He could not succeed as incidents involving people of Koduru repeated time and again. It appears chances were remote now, as Mala would enter his life and she belonged to a place near Koduru. Many persons known to both their families might be encountered thereafter, he thought. Now, it might fall to him to change his approach to past contacts and classmates of Koduru.

* * *

Ashok and Mohan reached Koduru. They picked up Ashok's parents and his sister Bala and Jaggu and proceeded to Rajolu, Mala's place. They reached there by seven in the evening and were received in the front hall by Mr. Narender, his wife and son Sagar. After a few moments Mohan's parents joined them. Ashok's mother introduced Bala and Jaggu to them.

They were served refreshments and drinks.

After a while, Mala accompanied by her sister Neelima entered the hall.

Mr. Narender introduced his daughters Malathi and Neelima to the visitors.

He said "Malathi is known as Mala, and you already saw Sagar my son. Neelima my first daughter is married recently."

Malathi greeted the parents of Ashok and smiled to Bala as Ashok introduced her.

Mohan said "Malathi is working as a software professional at Vizag."

They had a talk of local affairs and about Koduru and Rajolu.

Mohan, Ashok and Sagar and his sisters had their conversation in low key keeping the seniors off the subjects. Bala joined them.

After an hour, Mr. Krishnarao said they will inform the suitable dates for marriage, after consulting the *pandits*. Then they could fix a date suitable to both the families.

After the formalities Ashok left for home with his family.

* * *

On the way, while in the car, Ashok's mom said "They are rich families, big houses, lands and all that."

She expressed indirectly her doubts about the treatment they would get latter.

Bala said "Mom, nowadays after marriage, unless you take extra care the relationships might fade away."

She said so to tease her brother, Ashok.

Ashok laughed and said "Not everyone, my dear sister. For example, I am an exception to that. Take it from me."

He took Jaggu in to a close hug, as if to prove himself.

They all laughed.

His dad said "In many middleclass families, in one generation they become rich and remain so for some time. As long as the off-spring could maintain the tempo they continue to be rich. If some members become incapable or lazy, the riches dwindle and next generation sees the slide down. Again, it may pick up after one or two generations. In the families of big business people, they take care to keep the main core of wealth not mishandled and they continue to be rich except for one or two odd guys."

Ashok agreed with that logic and said "Yes, dad you analysed the position clearly."

His father continued "But Ashok, compare this with political families. The prosperity mostly depends on the ingenuity of the existing leadership and their relationship with people and their local leaders."

Ashok said "Yes, dad, that is entirely a different story and difficult to analyse with various odd factors.

They reached home.

After getting down the car, Ashok looked up at their house and said "Dad, I think we must modernise this house, to accommodate more visitors on special occasions."

His dad "It is O.K., Ashok. We can adjust. We have been living in this and can continue for some more years."

His mom said "The other day those relatives came from Rajolu and it was not alright to make them adjust in small space. It was embarrassing."

Ashok said "O.K., what I think, we can make some changes without affecting the main house. In front of the house we can make a hall and a staircase to go upstairs. In the first floor, there will be a hall and two bedrooms on either side. By these changes the basic view will not change and conforms to dad's wish."

His dad said "But to tell you frankly, I don't want to look rich suddenly after all these years of modest living."

Ashok "Dad, I understand that and will not go against your wish. It will be done accordingly and I will show the plans before doing any changes. O.K."

* * *

Now it was the turn of Mala, full name Malathi, to call Ashok for a date at a place to spend good time, as he called it. Now that the marriage had been fixed but for the date yet and also that Ashok had become familiar and turned out to be a boy from neighbourhood, she thought she could meet her fiancé again.

She called "Hi, Ashok, is it O.K. if we meet at some place once again?"

"Yes. Certainly. Right now I am busy with the production schedule. But you can meet me at factory office freely. That is one way to familiarise yourself with this office location too. Will you please come for lunch?"

"Your canteen lunches?"

"No. no. I get lunch daily from my home kitchen. You would like it. I will send car for you when you are ready."

"O.K., after one thirty, I will be ready."

"Sure."

* * *

Mala reached the factory of Ashok, Maxima Productions, at Bheemunipatnam. The factory building occupied only half of the area available. They maintained nice greenery and flower plants around. There were some well grown trees too around the compound wall. Mala looked around appreciatively.

Mala and Ashok sat in the office room. They had pleasant exchanges for a long time.

After sometime, the office boy came to inform that lunch was ready. They moved to the anteroom.

After gulping a few helpings, Mala said "Your home kitchen food is very good. I got bored eating the hostel food."

"The appreciation would go to Nair, our chef at home."

After lunch, Ashok asked her if she would like to see the factory.

She said "I already saw the landscape from the front. It is a good view. But it would be enjoyable to stroll around in the cool ambience of the evenings."

"O.K. that is for some other day and you would then come for evening snacks?"

He asked.

She agreed for another visit.

It was four by then and Mala wanted to go back. Ashok arranged the car for her.

* * *

Ashok was prompt in getting a blueprint made for the changes to be made in the old house at Koduru. And he kept in mind his father's requirement of, minimum changes, in the existing front elevation.

The elevation was not changed except for the hall in the front and staircase beside it. On the first floor the hall and two bedrooms on either side were at the backside. Pillars were laid wherever necessary to boost the strength of the structure. Work began right-earnest. Mr. Krishnarao did not object to the plan as it would not alter the basic structure of the ancestral building made by his father.

Ashok used to visit his native town, once in two weeks, on the weekends. The contractor was a known person to the family. So not much supervision was needed. As per the contractor, the estimated construction time for completion was three months.

* * *

12

Construction work of the new factory was completed.

Ashok and Mohan were supervising the installation of the machinery. As it was a continuous process plant, the assembly of the machinery was stringently checked. Otherwise, during the process if any part of the machinery was stuck the entire process comes to a halt. The process of production was explained to them, by the foreman.

The cut planks of wood of standard sizes introduced in the first section get their surfaces and four edges cleaned and smoothened. Then the planks in horizontal position, go to the application section, where their top and bottom surfaces get application of a special material. They then go to the next section, where each of them, get two additional planks of same size attached to the top and bottom surfaces. In the next section the treated triple-plank gets pressed and finished with a special material applied on all edges to give them the strength to withstand the vagaries of atmospheric variations of temperature and moisture. Then the triple-plank goes for drying and then to finished goods section.

The assembly of machinery was going on.

Mohan now had an occasion to speak to Ashok privately.

Mohan said "Ashok I want to tell you something, which I was hesitating to tell till now. Myself and Ramya had been pursuing surrogacy for getting children. Today, we came to know from the doctor that the process has become successful."

Ashok patted Mohan on the back and smiled happily.

He said "I am glad about this news."

Mohan continued "We chose a surrogate mother and Dr. Suguna is a friend of Ramya. She was of good help. We wanted to tell only when it succeeds."

"That is O.K., and fine" Ashok said.

The foreman called them again to check the assembled machinery.

* * *

The date for the marriage of Ashok was fixed to be 25th of October. The venue was the house of the bride at Rajolu.

Ashok during one of his visits to Koduru, got the invitation card drafted and designed there only and took the consent of his parents.

When the cards were printed and delivered to them, they began sending them to relatives and friends by post.

Ashok's paternal uncle, father of Subbu and one aunt were at Koduru only. Another paternal aunt was at Vijayawada. One maternal aunt was at Hyderabad. Many other relative's addresses were collected and cards were posted.

* * *

At the new Perfect Wood Products factory site, Bhumunipatnam, Mohan and Ashok were busy checking the receipt of raw materials, wooden planks and other materials. The other materials which go with the wooden planks were delivered in wooden boxes well packed to be safe from moisture and heat.

The go-downs were filled with the materials under the supervision of the store keeper, Mr. Pillai. The foreman Mr. Raman was helping him in checking the quality.

The trial production was planned on a day after a fortnight. By that time the assistant foreman and a dozen workmen would report.

Security personnel to take care of the factory premises round the clock were in place already.

When they became free, Mohan asked Ashok "Ashok, how are the preparations for marriage going on?"

Ashok smiled "It is going on, a continuous process you know. In such functions, ladies takeover more responsibilities. Because, it is about offering of gifts and clothes to the other party and relatives. Purchase of gold and silver ornaments is another important aspect of marriage. Regarding marriage ritual part, parents arrange the *purohit* and he brings all the required materials and we pay him. Bridegroom's reception party comes much later."

Mohan "How about your preparation, dresses all that?"

Ashok "I am not very particular about that."

Mohan smiled and said "What, Ashok, you must get new suits for the marriage, reception and so on."

Ashok smiles "O.K., I will get that."

Mohan "You get two suits at least. In fact, this is the occasion, when you get good dresses stitched."

Ashok "O.K., brother, I will do that. Thank you."

* * *

Ashok went to Visakha Dress Makers at R.K. Nagar.

It was a popular place and regularly they get orders from Navy officials.

That was a big shop, with annexures available for attending to each customer separately, while privacy was maintained.

Ashok went in and met the manager. He called a boy and asked him to take Ashok in to one of the enclosure attended to by a specified tailor.

Ashok saw a middle-aged man in the enclosure who smiled and greeted him. He appeared to have recognised Ashok.

He said "Ashok babu, do you remember me. I was at Koduru, in the early age. Later I got trained and taken on rolls here."

Ashok looked up, at him again and recognised him. He knew Ashok's background at Koduru. He used to stitch pants for Ashok after making adjustments to his father's old pants.

Ashok felt bad at first, but he became composed at once and smiled.

He said "How can I forget you. We know each other. You were so helpful to us in those days. You were a young boy then. I don't remember your name."

The tailor said "I am Balayya, sir. Thank you, sir."

He was very courteous and did not show any sign of disrespect or sarcasm.

After taking measurements, Balayya smiled and said that he would deliver the suits within two weeks.

Ashok getting accustomed to such incidents by now, laughed and told Balayya "Mr. Balayya, these are for my marriage. I would like you to be present at my marriage at Rajolu."

He then gave him his card.

Balayya thanked him and expressed joy at the growth in status of Ashok and also for his marriage.

Ashok felt relieved of the burden of resentment for the incident of facing one more Koduru person, after the pleasant ending of the incident.

* * *

On the day of the first trial run, the foreman planned for one shift of eight hours. Each cycle took one hour. By evening the finished products were ready for inspection. The foreman and assistant foreman made the process smooth.

Ashok and Mohan checked some units of the product, and concurred with opinion of the foreman that the product appeared to be normal. Only the machine check for the quality control was remaining. The quality control machine was not technically approved by the supplier's agent. That was posted for that weekend, when the agent would be present.

The trial run would be going on for two weeks and before that quality control part would be in place.

At the end of the month representatives of the construction company who would be buying the product and the agent of the dealers would be present and inspect the products.

* * *

13

On the day of the marriage, Mr. Narender arranged a bus at Koduru for the family and relatives of the groom, to reach Rajolu in the evening. Marriage was at nine on the morning of next day.

All the relatives of Ashok were assembled at the houses of Ashok and his uncle, Mr. Narasimharao. At Ashok's house the guests were entertained by his sister Bala and her husband Venkat during their stay there. The guests at Subbu's house were taken care of by Subbu and his wife Ramani.

The bus started at six in the evening and reached the hall arranged by Mr. Narender for the groom's party to stay for the night at Rajolu. Sagar guided and supervised the smooth transition of the groom's party and their luggage to the hall.

The pre-marriage dinner was arranged at Mr. Narender's house in the ground floor. For the groom and his parents, dinner was brought to the hall where they stayed for the night.

Mohan was with Ashok most of the time.

* * *

Next day, the preparations for marriage began very early in the morning.

The marriage was a grand occasion attended by all relatives and friends of both the bride and groom.

Morning refreshments and coffee and tea were served to all guests at the ground floor hall.

The bride and groom occupied their seats on the dais, set in floral decorations. The priest sat at a side to the bride and groom. Women relatives of the bride and groom nestled close to them. Bala the groom's sister and Subbu's wife Ramani were among them behind the groom. And Vani and Neelima were next to Malathi, the bride. The entire scene around the groom and bride looked like a colourful painting with various coloured *sarees* of multiple designs of different regions of the country at one place. The fragrances emanating from the enthusiastic guests wafted all around.

The priest began uttering the invocation *mantras* and the *Vedic* ritual began with the occasional drumbeats and *shehnai* of the musicians, who sat on a raised platform at a distance from the dais.

The first step of the marriage—placing of jaggery and other grains on the heads of each other by the groom and bride at the utterance of *mantras* by priests and the blaring of drums and music by the musicians was accomplished at the fixed auspicious time.

The next step was tying of turmeric thread carrying two pieces golden talisman around the neck of the bride by the groom. It was a commitment to the bride by the groom to abide by *sastras* to be with her lifelong with loyalty and attachment. It was also a perpetual symbol of mutual trust and togetherness. Ashok fulfilled this with drums and music blaring and *mantras* of the priest resounding.

Next in the schedule was pouring of fistfuls of turmeric touched rice on each other's heads by the groom and bride. This brings the lighter side of the program too, as both the bride and groom were encouraged by their respective relatives to show one-upmanship, by pouring the rice faster. Bala and Ramani pushed Ashok forward to pour the turmeric rice on the bride. Not to be left behind Vani and Neelima joined hands to encourage bride to take the lead. There was explosive merriment all around.

In fact, this ritual might signify the mutual respect shown by the bride and groom. And on the other hand, it was as if they are blessing each other, with the sanctified rice. We know, elderly persons shower turmeric rice on youngsters as an act of blessing. Again, the deities are always respected by placing turmeric rice on them to the chanting of *mantras* in all rituals. It also helps in developing intimacy with each other.

The friends and relatives wished the couple with long and happy married life, while offering gifts.

The marriage ritual comes to an end with the final function of the transferring bride's well-being in to the safe hands of the in-laws. The bride keeps up the legacy of the family to which she now belongs and upholds it with grace and dignity. She maintains the traditions of respect and wealth of the new family.

They were all entertained with multiple course lunch in the ground floor decorated hall. Six rows of fifty plus in each row, buzzed with the guests enjoying the feast with intimate conversations with each other about the marriage. The men served varieties of dishes in uniform with enthusiasm and urgency.

* * *

After the evening tea and snacks, many in the groom's party got ready to go to their places.

The bride and the groom with his family left the bride's home to reach theirs after the usual formalities.

The bride was accompanied by her sister and her cousin.

Ashok' house was already kept tidy, and colourful, with the construction work halted temporarily.

* * *

The bride and groom stayed for three days at Ashok's house.

Mala and her sister were not accustomed to live in places where the facilities were limited. They both shared their dissatisfaction with each other, but did not complain with Ashok or anyone else. Ashok and his mother understood their difficulty, but could not help it. Ashok explained to Mala that once the upstairs portion work was done, they can freely move around and have better facilities. That happens when they visit his parents there. At Vizag the situation would be different and nothing to complain there.

Ashok used his stay there to supervise the construction work. The upstairs work was getting finished, final coat of plaster being done. It would take three more weeks to finish the painting and electrical and plumbing work.

On one of those days, when he was standing outside the house, a scooter rider stopped near the house.

The scooter rider called aloud and said "Hi, Ashok, how are you? Your house is looking good now."

Ashok turned around to see his high schoolmate, Dinakar, whom he wanted to refer to as D only.

Ashok smiled and said "Yes, I am fine."

D smiled back and said "You are married now. I came to know."

He now put the scooter on stand and came forward to talk.

Ashok watched him with full attention, of course, he was not happy for this encounter. Dinakar became older to his age and appeared not in good shape financially, his dress indicated so.

With bent head and low voice Dinakar asked Ashok "Friend, can I get some job in your company. I am in need of help."

Ashok was touched by his supplication and tapped him on shoulder reassuringly and said "You get me your resume, I will check where I can fix you."

Dinakar looked up and smiled "Thanks Ashok. I know you are owner of a successful company. I came to know today only that you are here. I was in fact, hesitating to approach you."

And then he again thanked him and said "I will come to you tomorrow with the resume."

It was already noon. Ashok said "O.K."

Dinakar left him, with a smile of satisfaction on his face.

Ashok felt happy that he could help someone known to him. It was a surprise to him that some local people of his younger days knew about him and his present status. That gave him a sense satisfaction and reassurance and blew away the clouds of bad memories of the past.

* * *

Next day in the morning Dinakar came to Ashok, paid his respects and gave him his resume. He left him with one more request for help and gave his phone number written on a paper.

After an hour to this, Ashok's teacher in the school Mr. Raghavaiah came to his house. He was a colleague of Ashok's father, Mr. Krishnarao. They talked about the old times for a long time in the front room. Mr. Raghavaiah sought the help of Ashok to get a job for his son, who had a degree in commerce.

His dad called Ashok and told him about Mr. Raghavaiah's requirement. Ashok greeted his teacher and asked him to send the bio-data of his son. He promised that he would certainly fix him in his new company.

Ashok found himself to be liked by the residents of Koduru, who he hitherto thought never gave him any regard. Now he reconciled himself with the thought that in childhood it might happen thus to many people. That put him in good spirits.

Two days later, in the evening, his brother-in-law Sagar came to his house to invite him to their house, at Rajolu. That was a formality to take the groom and bride for three days at the house of groom's father-in-law.

Sagar formally requested the parents of Ashok to send the bride and groom to their house.

* * *

With due formalities the groom and bride with her companions were taken from bride's-in-laws house to groom's-in-laws place. Bala, sister of Ashok and her son Jaggu accompanied Ashok.

Many close relatives of the bride again visited the newlyweds at Rajolu.

On the third day Mohan and Ramya came to bride's house and invited them for lunch at their house.

The lunch was arranged in the upstairs terrace hall. The open place gave good view and cool breeze from the lake.

The groom and bride left them in the evening to bride's place.

Next day with all formalities the bride was sent to groom's house for a happy married life.

* * *

14

Finally, Ashok and Mala reached their own home at Vizag accompanied by Ashok's parents and Bala and Jaggu.

With Nair's best dishes they enjoyed the days at the city house of Ashok.

One day, Ashok took Mala and his parents and sister to the new factory at Bheemunipatnam. They went inside the factory. As it was no-work day, there was no noise to disturb them. Ashok explained the process in detail. Then they all went around the factory. The gardener made the backside of the factory like a park with flower plants in bloom and ornamental shrubs. Some wooden benches were fixed among them beside pathways. The trees planted along the compound wall, were yet to grow big.

Ashok's parents and sister went back to Koduru after two days.

One evening, Mohan and Ramya visited the newlyweds. They stayed for the dinner.

Ramya appreciated the food prepared by Nair.

She said "I only heard of this from Mohan before. Now I have direct experience of Mr. Nair's expertise."

Nair made his special pudding, which was liked by all.

* * *

The office building at the new factory was ready with all furniture and fittings.

Ashok and Mohan sat in the conference room. They reviewed the progress.

The trial production was accepted by the warehouse supervisor after checking on the quality control machine. The regular production of one shift for day was already finished for two weeks.

Orders for buying were received from Neeladri Construction Company for six months and three months production from the dealers. Accordingly, the production schedule was made.

They had already recruited staff for stores, warehouse and factory for one shift. The total strength of staff reached fifty. Administration and accounting and helpers were ten more members. There is a manager now by name Ramesh, taking care of office.

Mohan could bestow more time at the factory as his other activity of wood business had already been well established and in place since the time of forefathers.

Ashok could come thrice a week to the new factory and they allotted work to themselves accordingly.

Ashok said "Mohan, we have to get more orders now. We have to advertise in popular newspapers."

Mohan "Yes, we could also write to construction companies with brochures highlighting the cost savings by using planks in the place of walls."

Ashok "That's right. The demand depends on popularising the utility value. We call the Manager to explain the action on his part. He can start on advertisement and writing letters to construction companies."

Mohan "Yes."

He pressed the number of the Manager on intercom and asked him to come to conference room.

After Mr. Ramesh came and occupied his seat, Ashok said "Mr. Ramesh, we have stabilized on production now. We have to improve the demand from users. Next step is to advertise in popular newspapers. You can please make a draft and we can finalize that. We can also write to construction companies along with a brochure. The brochure could contain the matter given in the newspaper advertisements. Please make the drafts and we will sit again for finalizing."

Mohan said "Mr. Ramesh we will finish this work during this week."

Ramesh said "Yes, sir."

The helper boy brought coffee for them.

After coffee the manager left.

Ashok too left after some time to reach his factory and Mohan walked in to the factory while the work was going on.

* * *

Ramya called Mala and told "Hi Mala, my parents want to come to your house and see you newlyweds. They could not come to your marriage, as they were not here."

Mala smiled and said "Certainly. They are welcome and we will have their blessings."

Ramya "Tomorrow evening they want to come as it is Saturday. Ashok will also be free, I think."

Mala "Yes. We will await your parents and also you and Mohan."

Ramya said "Thanks Mala, of course Mohan and I will accompany them."

Mala "You are all staying for dinner, of course."

Ramya "That depends on my parents. They are older people you know."

Mala "O.K. As you please."

* * *

Next day, in the evening, Ramya, her parents and Mohan reached Ashok's place.

They brought dresses for the newlyweds and a gift packet of household-articles.

Mala insisted on them to stay for dinner.

They agreed.

Ramya's father liked the food.

He said "I have been going on to different countries and I can boldly say Mr. Nair's food is exceptional. I feel like taking him away from you to my house."

He laughed loudly accompanied by the chorus of laughters of others.

Ramya's mother agreed with him and addressing Nair, she said "Yes, yes, Mr. Nair, you please visit us at least once a week. That too when Ramya's father is here."

She laughed again.

Ashok said with a smile "Certainly, sir, you can take him from us, sometimes."

Nair was smiling happily for the accolades. But it was not new for him to get appreciated where ever he works. He was sober and the appreciation did not go to his head any time.

* * *

At their home, Mala and Ashok were enjoying the holiday.

Mala said with a smile "Today being Sunday, you are free and at my disposal, O.K."

Ashok smiled and putting his hand around her, who was sitting next to her in the hall, said

"Tell me dear, what is my duty today, being a holiday?"

"Nothing difficult, we will go to a restaurant for dinner in the evening,"

"Certainly, anywhere you say."

They were married recently and the newly joined life-partner wanted to enjoy the city life together.

* * *

After six in the evening, Ashok and Mala readied to go to the Visakha three-star Restaurant, a popular elite restaurant.

After reaching the restaurant, Ashok sent the driver away, asking him to come again only after a call from him.

They entered the restaurant-hall, hand in hand smiling with happiness, left to themselves free after a long time. It was a large well-furnished place with subdued lighting. They sat at one of the middle tables.

They felt relaxed, after so many days of hectic get-together-parties with relatives and friends after marriage.

Ashok asked her "How do you feel the life at Vizag now after marriage."

Mala with a huge smile "Great, really great. Before marriage I was living with roommates in hostel reluctantly though. Lot of adjustment was needed there. Any one might get bad feelings even for a small unintended action or word. We had to live in a sensitive way. Now I am free and living with a person I love and loved by. All life left to myself with full freedom."

Ashok "So much feeling. You are an artist. Someone told me that you paint well and I have yet to see those paintings. But you painted your life then and now in words so beautifully."

They ordered the dishes liked by each and also liked together. They glanced around and found that the hall was almost full.

They enjoyed the food, though they were accustomed to Nair's lip-smacking varieties at home.

After an hour and half, they paid the bill and walked out in to the open yard set with flower pots and chairs to relax, as well as for waiting.

Ashok and Mala sat at a side, not crowded.

After sometime he called the driver on phone.

Now, he heard laughter from one side at a distance. He looked at that side and found a familiar face of Koduru. That was his schoolmate, whose name he could not get readily. He was sitting next to a lady, might be his wife. They turned their eyes away when he looked at them.

The driver called back, to tell his availability outside.

Ashok told Mala that his schoolmate was there at that side and that they would meet them, as a courtesy. Ashok wanted to lessen the burden of brooding about their laughter later, if aimed at him or not.

Ashok and Mala walked to them and stood close to them. There was sufficient light to recognise each other. He smiled and extended his hand to his assumed to be schoolmate.

That person smiled and readily got up and took Ashok's hand in his. He then told his wife, the lady beside him, that was his schoolmate.

Ashok said "I am Ashok, you are…."

He stopped there.

The other person said "Ashok, I am Jnan, Jnana Sundaram. This is my wife Mani. And Mani this is my school mate Ashok.

Mala too introduced herself.

Then they stood there for some time and talked about each other.

After Ashok received another call from his driver, he took leave of them after courteous greetings.

Ashok walked out of the restaurant with Mala, while explaining to her, his sensitive nature and childhood background without any reservations. His mind became clear and peaceful now.

Mala said "Ashok, that happens in many families. One generation they rise high and after some years they may come down in riches. There is nothing to feel bad about that."

Ashok "Yes, what you said is right."

He then remembered his father's comments on the same line, sometime back while they were returning to Koduru from Rajolu after a visit to Mr. Narender's house.

* * *

15

Mrs. Jaya delivered a female baby. The doctor allowed Ramya to take the baby home after the mandated period for surrogate deliveries. They were given directions to take care of the baby. Dr. Suguna assured Ramya that she would always be available for her baby first and she could call her anytime without hesitation.

After a few days, Mohan and Ramya celebrated the cradle ceremony of the baby grandly at their home in Vizag. They invited only close relatives and friends to avoid any unpleasant comments by some over-enthusiastic people. Ashok and Mala attended the function. Ashok's parents informed Mohan that they would come after attending a marriage in the city.

Mohan's house located at S' Dhara was built by his father long back in a big plot of thousand yards. The house appeared old, but had all the modern features.

They covered a part of the area in front of the house with large tarpaulin to facilitate its usage for the function. The main function was performed in the large front hall of the house. The pundits performed the naming function with all the rituals. Ramya's and Mohan's parents attended the function with their close friends and relatives. Mohan's sister Vani was there with her husband Sankar. They came from U.S.A. a couple of days back for the function. Vani was busy meeting their relatives there and enquiring about their welfare. While Ramya sat with Mohan attending to the rituals, Vani took over the responsibility of taking care of relatives and friends.

Vani asked Mala, her cousin to help her in attending to the guests. Ashok sat with Mala in the first row watching the ceremony at close quarters.

Ashok's parents came at the time of naming the baby. Mohan took Mr. Krishnarao to the place where his and Ramya's parents were sitting and made a place for him there. Mohan's father smiled and greeted Mr. Krishnarao. He introduced him to Ramya's father, who just smiled with conspicuous lack of courtesy. He knew Mr. Krishnarao was just a school teacher and does not require a special attention. But Mr. Krishnarao greeted him before sitting amongst them. Mohan felt bad but could not dispel the unpleasantness. Ashok was watching the scene from a distance. He knew that status counts very much in society and not character. He had umpteen such incidents in his life already.

Ashok's mother too had similar experience among the ladies of elite. They all had rich family background. She already knew this when she visited Ashok's father-in-law's and his brother's houses at Rajolu. But she knew some ladies' nature and did not get disheartened at all. She kept smiling and enjoyed the function.

Ramya took the blessings of Ashok's parents for the child. She gave them equal respect as due to Mohan's parents. Mala introduced her in-laws to all known friends and relatives in the gathering.

Lunch was served in the large facility in front of the house with all the formality.

* * *

16

It was a big gathering of ladies of the families of Mohan and Ashok.

Baby-shower function of Neelima, sister of Mala. It was seventh month of pregnancy for Neelima.

Mala came to parent's house at Rajolu three days before. Mohan and Ramya with the baby came a day before the function. They were invited by Mr. Narender and his wife and they insisted on their presence in the function. Mr. Narender considered the function important as it is the first grandchild in his family.

The hall in the first floor was brightly lit in coloured lights and the ladies in beautiful *sarees* were shuttling around as it was mainly a ladies' function. Neelima sat in a specially brought big chair surrounded by her mother, in-laws, sister Mala and Ramya. Neelima was dressed up gorgeously with a beautiful *saree*, colourful bangles and flowers.

It appeared a function of cheer and abundance.

Neelima's husband Shyam was standing aside watching the function with a shy smile on his face as not many males were in attendance.

After completing the formalities, the gathering beelined to the dining hall as it culminated in a feast for all family members, relatives and friends.

Mohan and his family and Ashok with his parents attended the dinner. Mala was taking care of the guests.

After dinner Mala and Ramya went in to central hall which had two bedrooms on either side. It was fully furnished. Ramya saw a few beautiful paintings among a number of enlarged family photos.

Ramya stopped in front of a painting of the building in which they were there now. It was a beautiful landscape. It was drawn on a big canvas featuring the front elevation of that building. It included the park with plants and trees around.

Ramya asked "Such a beautiful painting. Who is the artist?"

Mala "I only did that during my holidays during college days."

Ramya moved to the next painting skipping the family photos in between. It was a landscape depicting Nallacheruvu of the town. The lake with boats and some tourists surrounded by trees was very much sitting there in place.

Ramya said with elation "How about this?"

"These paintings I made now and then. That is my hobby." She said.

Ramya with surprise and appreciation "My goodness. You are such a good artist. These should have been put up in an exhibition by now."

Mala laughed and expressed her joy for the recognition of her talent.

Ramya continued "We must do something about this. This talent should not go unrecognised simply because the artist is modest."

* * *

Mala continued to work in the software company. Ashok did not object her for a few months. Now that the 'Perfect Wood Products' had started working and become successful, he asked her if she could participate in managing the company. He said he could not attend to the work of both the companies. Of course, Mohan was also doing the work of the new company. The necessity of more persons became urgent in view of the expansion plans for another factory. The demand for more new wood products had increased. More dealers wanted to keep stocks of the new wood products. The growth in demand was due the realization of consumers that the new wood products would save cost of construction. The added advantage was that they could save time in construction too. The sales promotion measures adopted by the company, like advertisements and follow up with construction companies and dealers by the salesmen, pushed up the demand fast.

* * *

Ashok took the help of Rajesh in getting permissions for starting another factory near the existing one. They planned to purchase a few acres of land adjacent to the industrial area. With great persuasion, Rajesh could secure the permission with the political influence of an M.P. of the district. Rajesh had bargained with huge amount of push money to get the work done.

Ashok and Mohan had bargained for two and half acres of land in the vicinity in advance.

* * *

17

Ramya's father could not continue to tour abroad due to his advancing age. He sought the help of Mohan to ease his work load. Ramya was already busy with the business affairs of the company locally. Thus, Mohan's participation in the work of new wood company became restricted now. Mala had to take the responsibility of Mohan to some extent. But that did not solve the problem fully.

Mohan asked Ashok "In the present situation, we must think of other members of our families to share the responsibility."

Ashok "My father is not active enough to take any work now."

Mohan "Of course, that is right. My father too is no good. But I suggest why don't you explore the possibility of Mr. Venkat, your brother-in-law."

Ashok smiled and said, "I have not thought about that. If only he leaves that job of his, in which he was stuck up for about two decades, that would be good."

Mohan too smiled "Yes, that would be ideal. He can take this responsibility easily with his experience at senior level already for many years."

Ashok "I will talk to him. But it must be very tactical way because it will not be easy for him to forego that big-city life and comfortable position in the company."

Mohan "I agree. If you don't mind my telling this, you offer him good compensation and also some shares in the company. And also tell him about his future life with parents and own people."

Ashok laughed loudly "My goodness, you speak like a politician. I will take that line, now that you only suggested these measures. I cannot offer all these without your concurrence."

Mohan "What I said is reasonable, because a person like that you cannot get without sufficient compensation. And above all, he is one of our own families."

Ashok smiled and said "I will do that."

* * *

On Ramya's suggestion, Mala wanted to use her free time for painting. But Ashok now burdened with extra work, insisted on her to share his work at the factory. With that she had to resign her job and started to go to the new wood company.

* * *

During one of his visits to Koduru, Ashok's mother asked him why she had not become a grandmother yet.

At first, he could not make out the meaning.

Then he laughed and said "Mom. It is all God's grace.

His mom said "NO, no, Mala's sister Neelima is already a mother now."

That evening, Ashok told Mala about this. Mala said they should not ignore this suggestion, as other people too would begin to talk about this.

Afterwards, when he was alone in the balcony watching the stars in the blue sky, Ashok, pondered over his life and how fast things were moving from one incident to another.

Next day in the morning, Ashok and Mala left for Vizag after two days trip to Koduru.

* * *

After a few days, Ashok's father called him and told that housing board had made plots at Koduru and he had applied for one plot and got it sanctioned. He said they could make another house in that plot. Ashok was surprised to see the change in his father's stance. He used to say modest living and all that. Now he was prepared to acquire more properties for the family. He knew that Venkat was being called to Vizag for taking up job at the new wood company.

Ashok smiled and said "Dad, go for a big plot of land, so that we can have moving space around."

His dad "Ashok, the plots are three hundred yards each in size. No bigger plots were made."

Ashok "Dad, then go for three plots adjacent to each other."

His dad "O.K. I will do that. Send the money in to my account."

"O.K. dad."

* * *

After a week, Ashok's dad called him "Ashok, I paid for two plots. Third plot adjacent to them was bought by Subbu already. Other side plot not available. But if I give my already paid plot to Subbu, he may forego the plot adjacent to our two plots"

"Yes, dad, that is a good idea, go ahead. Do you want me to talk to him?"

"Not necessary, he will consider my necessity."

* * *

Sometime later, Ashok called his dad "Dad, Subbu called me and told that he had given his plot to you as we wanted. He actually called me to ask for a job for his brother-in-law, Chandu, and I said o.k. quid pro quo, dad."

"O.K. son, yes. Subbu agreed, whatever reason may be there. But he was helpful to me."

At last, Mr. Krishnarao got three plots of a total site of nine hundred yards, registered in his name.

* * *

Ashok called sister Bala "Hi sister, how are you people? I want to talk to brother-in-law."

"Yes, Brother. We are fine. He is here."

Venkat laughed and said "Hi, Ashok. When is the party for the arrival of baby?"

"For that there is time, brother in law, may be two months. Bala knows. Apart that, we urgently need a qualified man as the head of the new factory."

"You advertise with requirements. Nowadays no problem for getting good men."

"We want an experienced person."

"Yes. Wait, you would get such a person if you pay him well."

"How much do you think we have to pay to get such a person to manage independently as C.E.O.?"

"May be twenty-five lakhs per annum plus house, etc."

"That's it. I request you to consider this as offer from our company to you, my dear brother in law."

"My goodness. It is a shock. Are you serious? Why is this? Don't you get someone for this?"

"Brother-in-law, this is a position of Responsibility plus Reliability and Retention for a long period—R3."

"But I have to think about this. It takes time. It is a serious matter, to shift from an established job and place."

"Brother-in-law, Mohan is busy now with his father-in-law's business. We need you. Mohan suggested this. He said shares in the new company could be offered so as to compensate the seniority you forego in your present position. And a house suitable to the position of a C.E.O. would be provided."

"That's O.K., Ashok, you talk to you sister too. She is accustomed to Mumbai city's life."

"O.K., I will convince her with the logic that she would be near her dad and mom. And same thing applies to you too."

Ashok laughed.

"Ashok. You are well prepared for this conversation of offer."

He continued,

“In case I accept, when am I to take the charge?’

“That is up to you, brother-in-law. But earlier the better, because I am overburdened now.”

“You know, I must get maximum benefits for my long service to this company. I have to bargain with management for that”

“Thank you. Brother-in-law, give the phone to sister.’

Ashok smiled and said to his sister “Bala, my dear sister, good news, you get ready to shift to Vizag. You will be near us in future.”

“When is this and why?’

“Brother-in-law will tell you. He becomes a C.E.O. at Vizag.”

He continued “O.K. Sister, bye.”

He kept the phone off.

* * *

18

Ashok called his dad and said "How are you both, dad? I am calling now just to tell you that we would make another building in the new plot. What do you say?"

His dad said "O.K., how is Malathi?"

"Her mother and dad will come here next week to take her to Rajolu for delivery."

"Good, good, now regarding the building, I want it simple with much site around to move freely. We could have plants and trees in that."

"Yes, Dad, as you please. But my idea is, we would go for loan and I will stand guarantee."

"Why. You don't have that much money now?"

"No. dad, it is about tax advantage. We get tax deduction. We can pay loan in instalments over a long period."

"O.K. I know an agent of L.I.C. we can take loan from them."

"I will be the collateral guarantor. And do you know that I asked brother-in-law to come over as C.E.O. for our new company. He agreed."

"Great. That is good news. When will they come here?"

"When he resigns that job at Mumbai. That must be in near future as we require him urgently."

"O.K., son."

* * *

Venkat resigned from his company at Mumbai and reached Vizag. He stayed with Bala and Jaggu at Ashok's house for two days. Then they left for Rajahmundry to meet Venkat's parents.

Ashok made arrangement with a friend whose bungalow at R.K. Puram was for lease. The lease at six lakhs per annum was done by the company. He then informed Venkat about this. He told him that he could work from home till his office building gets ready, that would be three months. One assistant would help him in his work there.

Ashok called Mr. Sunder and told him to send his son after a week to start working at the office of the company.

* * *

Mr. Krishnarao got a loan of fifty lakhs from L.I.C. for construction of the new building at Koduru. An amount of twenty lakhs was released as first instalment after fulfilling all the formalities.

He talked to Ashok and fixed up a date for ground breaking ceremony. He invited Venkat and his family to the function. Mohan and Ramya were invited by Ashok. Mr. Krishnarao invited his brother, father of Subbu and their family to the ceremony. As the ground breaking ceremony was a small formality, not many relatives or friends were invited. Mr. Narender and Mr. Dasaradh excused themselves for not being able to attend the function.

Mr. Narender later talked to Ashok and his father and fixed up the date of baby shower for Mala on the day next to ground breaking ceremony at Koduru to make it convenient for all of them to attend the function at Rajolu next day.

* * *

The ground breaking ceremony was done with a priest in attendance in the morning at seven. Mr. Krishnarao and his wife performed the *pooja*. They arranged breakfast after the ceremony.

They ordered lunch for the guests from a caterer at twelve noon.

Ashok, Venkat and his family were joined by Subbu and his family with his parents for the lunch. Mala remained with her parents at Rajolu. Mohan and Ramya too could not attend the function and they excused themselves.

The lunch was served under the tarpaulin covered enclosure for the guests, of course all relatives only.

After lunch, Mr. Krishnarao and all his family members reached the old but now renovated house. They had two bedrooms and hall in the first floor extra to keep them cosily well settled with all the modern facilities. A cook was arranged to take care of the food needs.

* * *

Next day, Mr. Krishnarao and all his family members proceeded to Rajolu for baby shower of Mala. Subbu and his family accompanied them. Ashok arranged a taxi car additionally for all of them to travel freely.

The baby shower ceremony was conducted as grand as that of Neelima, performed a few months before. Mohan and Ramya with the baby came down from his father's house accompanied by his parents.

Sagar took care of all the guests. His uncle Mr. Dasaradh commented the next big function would be the marriage of Sagar and he suggested to his brother to fix a girl early. Mr. Narender agreed to the suggestion. It was a lighter moment for them to enjoy and comment among them about the would-be bride.

Bala joined the womenfolk in the gala performance of the function, including singing and felicitation of Mala. After that when Mala was free, Ashok called her aside and sat with her for some time asking about her health and so on. Then he detailed her about the matters connected to the industries at Vizag and about the ground breaking ceremony at Koduru, at which she was felt missed.

The guests and friends were treated to a grand feast after the function.

After the dinner Ashok and his family excepting Mala proceeded to Koduru.

Mohan and his family left for their home. He said he planned to reach Vizag next day.

* * *

Next day early in the morning, Ashok and Venkat and his family started for Vizag. Venkat and his family stayed at the house of Ashok for two more days. In the evening, Ashok took Venkat and family to the leased house for a visit and to check the facilities available there. The building with one bedroom in ground floor and a hall and two bedrooms in the first floor, had a garden in the front and backyard. There were two office rooms and kitchen in the ground floor. To the left side of the building a big car shed was there. Bala checked the water supply and the running water connections were alright. All the three bathrooms had independent geysers. She checked the kitchen for cupboards and gas stove platforms. Ashok checked and found the air conditioners were functioning well. Ashok said the hired car would report to him early next day. All the luggage of Mr. Venkat would be shifted next morning to the new residence, he said.

Ashok asked Bala "Sister, do you want a cook?"

Bala smiled and said "No brother, I want to cook myself for my family."

Ashok said "Brother-in-law, there is an international school at a kilo meter distance. We can fix Jaggu there."

* * *

Venkat shifted to the new building after two days, when everything was arranged for a convenient living at the new place.

He started working from residence with one assistant, Sreedhar of Koduru.

* * *

19

Venkat started working from home. He however had to go to factory to supervise the construction work there. Sreedhar works in the office room, looking after the correspondence, filing and also attending to calls from visitors.

They had registered the new and second factory with the name 'Modern Building Materials.'

As the orders were piling up, they had to resort to two shifts work at the first factory. The third shift time was used for cleaning and restoration to avoid any breakdown and stoppage of production. As Mala was at her home, Ashok had to work extra hours, as he had to cope up with his Defence Department supplies which was his first mainstay. Mohan attended to the factory on two days of every week, as required by Ashok to give him a break. For the time being two shifts production took care of the existing orders.

The finance matters pertaining to payments to suppliers, collections from buyers and such matters of the first factory were looked after by Ashok.

All the finance matters and payments to contractors and other matters pertaining to the new factory were left to the care of Mr. Venkat as C.E.O.

When the new factory was registered, a new set of partners was made. Ashok and Mohan had concurred in selecting the partners. They wanted to include Malathi and Ramya as additional partners. But Ramya declined to share the responsibility, as she was busy with the existing work of his dad and could not spend any extra time in the new company. So, Mohan's father Mr. Dasaradh became a partner in her place.

In both the companies, the partners would decide policy matters pertaining to purchase, sales and finance. In the recruitment of factory staff and managerial staff they would be consulted in selection.

Selection of C.E.O.s would be the responsibility of the partners of the respective companies. For the first company, Ashok would act as the C.E.O. till a regular person was selected. Mohan was busy with his father-in-law's work and could not bestow more attention.

Once the clear picture of duties and responsibilities was drafted, the regular work became a routine.

* * *

Ashok called Mohan and said "Mohan, can you spend some time with me at the factory office. We will sit with Mr. Venkat to discuss about the work program and plans."

Mohan said "Certainly, Ashok. How can I ignore that company which is our brain child and is now growing fast? In fact, work at the new company is interesting and challenging. The established business matters like what I do now, are routine and does not require creative thinking but only responsible attention."

Ashok "Good, I too feel the same way about my other company."

Mohan "How is Mr. Venkat? Is he happy here?"

Ashok "No regrets, he appears to be enjoying the work and native place and people. So, when will you come over?"

Mohan "Any Sunday will be o.k. Next Sunday, is it O.K. for you and Mr. Venkat?'

Ashok "I will talk to him and let you know."

* * *

The three of them, two partners and a C.E.O. met at the factory. Mohan greeted Venkat and welcomed him to the new office.

They talked about the product, process and the demand. Venkat said after some discussion "Mr. Mohan, the demand appears to be good. The product is welcomed by the users. I have a suggestion to make regarding the process line. Before finalizing the factory construction, you could think of a second stream of process line beside the present one, so that we can expand the production without being taken unawares to face the surge in demand. So, we can plan for placing another stream next to the present one. If we don't have enough budget-provision we can plan for a skeletal structure for the time being to complete it in the future when the need arises."

Mohan said "Yes, Mr. Venkat, that is a good and timely suggestion. We actually missed this point while planning the present structure."

Ashok said "No problem, we can make some provision in place for that now. Regarding skeletal structure we will think of that when the need arises."

The trio had further discussions and the meeting came to an end.

* * *

After two months there was a second meeting of the trio, Ashok, Mohan and Venkat.

The building for the new factory was finished except for the interiors. They were to order machinery mostly to be fabricated and assembled. They had taken care, to leave sufficient place for future expansion by laying another stream of production line beside the present one. They estimated that one more month would be sufficient for interior work and to bring the machinery to working condition.

Venkat concurred with the estimated time of one month for beginning trial production.

After that two more weeks were required for reaching criticality for regular production.

Ashok said "we have to order the raw materials, once the go-down buildings are completed."

Venkat "It will take two weeks for the completion of go-down for raw materials and finished goods. The office building would be ready by next week and we can shift there. We need office staff and full security personnel by then."

Mohan "Mr. Venkat you can plan for recruiting office staff. Regarding security the same agency supplying the security personnel for the first factory could be approached unless you have an alternative plan."

Ashok "Regarding factory foreman, assistant foreman and workmen we have to advertise."

Venkat "I will take care of that. The details of qualification and experience, I could collect from factory one."

Mohan "Yes, sir, you can. Once the criticality is reached, we scan shift some orders to the new factory and the collections etc. independent of first factory."

Venkat "Yes, Mr. Mohan."

At this point of time, there was a phone call to Ashok from his father-in-law, Mr. Narender.

He said with a smile "Mr. Ashok, congratulations. Good news. You are blessed with a baby boy and Mala and baby are fine."

"Congratulations, father-in-law. I would like to speak to Mala."

His father-in-law gave the phone to Mala.

Ashok "Hi, Mala, congratulations to you. Thanks. I am in a meeting and I will speak to again."

Mala "O.K. Ashok."

The phone was kept off.

Ashok told his other members of the meeting about the good news.

Mohan and Venkat in one tone said "Congrats, Ashok."

Ashok laughed, joined by Mohan And Venkat.

They ordered for sweets and asked the manager to distribute them among the staff.

The three of them had one more of round of coffees.

* * *

20

Ashok reached Koduru next day in the morning. He picked up parents and went to Rajolu.

The baby and mother Mala were at the Nursing home. They took permission of the doctor and went in to the room. Mala was all smiles. The baby was asleep. Ashok and his mom went close to the crib and watched the baby.

The nurse who stood next to the crib, asked them not to touch the baby yet. Ashok's mother watching the baby smiling, with closed eyes, burst in to smiles herself.

Mr. Krishnarao said "A happy grandmother, she is."

His wife said still smiling "You have now climbed up to third generation, up from the second. A progeny had arrived now to carry forward the legacy."

Ashok's parents went out to give privacy to the couple.

Ashok spent some time with Mala.

She said "The doc said we can go home after the third day. The baby is healthy and weighs five pounds."

Ashok smiled and said "How do you feel?"

Mala said "I am fine. Why you did not bring Bala?"

Ashok said "Venkat was busy with his work. Bala cannot leave him alone. And Jaggu started going to school now."

Mala smiled and said "O.K. they can come for the cradle ceremony."

Ashok "When is that?"

Mala "On the twenty first day after birth of the baby."

Ashok touched the baby on the cheek. He smiled and touched Mala on the head. He waved a bye and went out of the room.

* * *

With active supervision by Venkat, the building construction including the interiors was completed. The go-down and office building were ready. The office was furnished and internet and other fittings were made. Venkat with Sreedhar shifted to the new office building. New recruits for office would be reported in a week thence. Machinery was ordered from the same company which supplied for the first factory. The supplier promised to assemble the machinery at once. The quality control machine would be in place by another week.

Venkat pursued the manpower supplier to send the personnel for interviews at the earliest. Ashok and Mohan told Venkat, that they would be available whenever he wants them to be present for interviews. The round the clock security was already in place.

* * *

After ten days the first batch of raw materials were received in the go-down.

Mohan and Ashok spent half days on every day for a week along with Venkat, to interview candidates for office and factory.

The foreman and assistant foreman were selected from local candidates. The workmen were taken from candidates from Orissa and also some local candidates.

For the office staff, Ashok picked two from Koduru and three from Vizag. Helpers were from Vizag only.

The date for trial run was fixed, by the time the quality control machine was received for testing.

The foreman of the first factory was asked to be present at the time of trial run of production.

Mr. Venkat, Ashok and Mohan watched the trial run of the product. Quality control check was found to be satisfactory. They felt that production could be started for one shift per day. This would ease the pressure on the first factory, which at present was running on extra shift to meet the orders for supply.

* * *

21

Mr. Narender invited Ashok, Venkat and Mohan with their families for the cradle ceremony of Malathi's son. He called Mr. Krishnarao and extended invite to him. Mr. Narender and his wife went to the house of his brother Mr. Dasaradh and invited them to attend the function.

Ashok, Venkat and his family started in his car on their way to Koduru to pick up Ashok's parents. Mr. Krishnarao went to his brother's house to ask if they would come with them to attend the function. He had already told him about cradle ceremony of their grandson and invited them. Subbu said they would come in his recently bought car.

Ashok started at eight in the morning and reached father-in-law's house by nine. They had breakfast there.

The function started at ten. The baby was put in the beautifully decorated cradle fixed in a stand of five feet height. A coloured rope was tied to the cradle to pull it back and forth. The priest uttered *mantras* and blessed the child. He asked the guests present to bless the child by putting turmeric rice on him. The ladies took turns to pull rope to move the cradle. After sometime the baby slept.

Ramya's parents came after some time. They exchanged greetings with the assembled elders.

There was a feast after completion of the function and offering of gifts to the child.

Except Ashok and his family all others left the place after the lunch. Ashok' mother and father had an occasion to fondle the baby. After that, Ashok took the baby in his arms and kissed him. Mala stood close to him and watched him with a smile. It was his sister Bala's turn to take the baby in arms and plant a delicate kiss on the cheek of the baby, while Jaggu tried to touch the baby.

After tea and snacks, Ashok and family started for Koduru.

By evening they reached Koduru and wanted to spend night there as next day was Sunday. Ashok planned to visit the building under construction on the next day.

* * *

When they reached the place of construction in the morning, after taking breakfast, it was ten. The structure was finished to the extent of columns and slabs for two floors. Ashok told the contractor that for non-load bearing walls to use wooden planks which would be sent by him later. But the contractor was not agreeable to that. He said wooden walls would wilt after some days and the building would lose its beauty and utility. Ashok told him that wooden planks were being used in many construction activities by Real estate companies. He even advised him to go for wooden planks in his future works. He said by using wooden planks the cost of construction becomes less and time would be saved. The contractor agreed at last but said that he would not be responsible for any damage or mishap later on. Ashok and Venkat laughed and said it would be alright. Ashok said the plastering work could be finished before fixing the wooden walls, which he would supply soon after reaching Vizag.

Ashok and Venkat then took measurements for the wooden planks required to be sent. The contractor assisted them in that.

Ashok told Venkat that the amount for the planks supplied to the building should be charged to his account in books. Venkat agreed to that.

By lunch time, they reached home. A few youths of the town were waiting for Ashok at his house. They came to request for jobs for them. Ashok thought Dinakar must have passed on the information. Two of them were graduates and the third one a matriculate. They brought their bio-data sheets. They told him that even if the jobs were not suitable to their qualifications, they were prepared to work. They hoped for elevation in future. Ashok took the bio-data sheets from them and told them they would get letters whenever any vacancies arise.

That evening Ashok and Venkat and his family started on their journey back to Vizag.

* * *

As the recruitment for staff goes on, Ashok reminded Mr. Venkat about the applications of the candidates from Koduru. Mr. Venkat told him that about the two graduate candidates, he would fix them in administrative office as trainee assistants, without interviews. Ashok agreed, as the training part would take care of their deficiencies if any. For matriculation candidates, Mr. Venkat said they could be selected after interview as trainee helpers, if suited.

* * *

The production in factory two, had been regularised now. The construction companies were lifting the stocks as when they require. They were not able to lift the entire quantity ordered by them. Added to this the dealers had no capacity to store the goods and they didn't have larger enough go-downs. The go-down space at factory two was not sufficient to store the ordered quantities if not lifted by the dealers. So Venkat said there was an urgency for one more go-down.

Ashok, Mohan and Venkat sat in a meeting to discuss the way out for this.

Mohan said "Can we get on lease the required space somewhere in the city?"

Venkat said "Mr. Mohan, I had already checked about that. Only long-term lease of go-downs of huge capacities are available. And of course, the lease amount would be huge. We require the space of small capacity and that too sporadically but not continuously."

Ashok said "So, what is the solution. We do not have that much money to go for a big go-down at this stage."

Mohan "That is right. We cannot afford to do that now and as you said for sporadic requirement."

Ashok "Can we go for loan?"

Venkat "They would not give loan for construction of go-down at this stage. Moreover interest would be a burden, without additional income. We cannot force the users to pay interest, either."

Mohan laughed and said" So, what is the magical solution, sir?"

Venkat "I considered about this for long and we must construct a go-down of small capacity just to take care of the present situation. But there must be scope for expansion without much extra money. That means, we could go for a small building with the convenience of making one more floor over that. That would take care of future needs. Presently we could also use the space if lying idle in the first factory on some notional charges."

Ashok said "That means we should plan for small building with good structure so that it could take a second floor over it. It could be a shed with strong structure."

Venkat "Exactly. That would cost us less. Moreover, we could use our own planks for walls."

Mohan "Right. That would be fine. Ashok, we could go for that. What?"

Ashok "I too agree."

Venkat "O.K., we will do that as early as possible."

The meeting concluded after coffees and easy talk for some time with personal anecdotes.

* * *

22

Mr. Krishnarao and his wife wanted to visit their daughter Mrs. Bala at Vizag and called her and told that. It was just an impulse to see the family of their daughter. They made a phone call to Ashok too. They started at once in a bus. Mr. Venkat told Ashok that he would pick them up from bus stand. He asked Ashok to join them for dinner so that he could spend time with his parents and sister.

Ashok's father told him, during the course of dinner that he must plan to bring Mala and baby during the first month of birth of the baby, otherwise they would not allow the baby and Mala to shift to in-laws place during second month. Then, he would have to wait for third month to bring them. Ashok asked his parents to stay with him till Mala and baby arrive and later to spend time with the baby. His mother laughed and said she would certainly stay with the grandson and son's family. His father smiled approvingly. His sister Bala too encouraged them to stay at Vizag so that she could meet them frequently. Jaggu too insisted them to stay at Vizag..

* * *

Mr. Krishnarao and his wife, Laxmi, spent two days at the daughter's house. On the third day, they wanted to go to Ashok's place. Mr. Venkat dropped them on his way to the factory.

That evening Mr. Krishnarao made a call to Mr. Narender and after pleasantries, told him to find an auspicious day for Malathi and Baby to come to husbands place. He told him that he was at Ashok's house at Vizag and that his wife was eager to play with their grandson. Mr. Narender smiled and said he would check with the *pandit* and come over there to drop their grandson and daughter-in-law at Vizag in the first month itself.

After informing Mr. Krishnarao that they would be prepared to come on Sunday, Mr. Narender and wife accompanied by Malathi and baby reached Ashok's place at Vizag in the morning. They brought all gifts and auspicious things to be sent with the daughter and the baby to in-law's house. The gifts meant for in-laws and clothes, to son-in-law and his sister Bala were brought by them. Ashok's mother and sister received the daughter-in-law and the baby with ceremonial routine.

Mr. Krishnarao called Mr. Venkat for lunch, as the in-laws of Ashok were present and they would like to go away in the evening to Rajolu. Ashok invited Mohan and Ramya for the lunch on the auspicious occasion.

They all had a feast with preparations by Mr. Nair.

Mr. Narender and wife left for Rajolu. Mohan and Ramya stayed up to tea time and then left for home.

After Mala's arrival with the baby, the grandparents had a nice time with them. After a week days, Mr. Krishnarao wanted to go to Koduru. But Mala and Ashok objected to their going so early, but his father said the building was in the finishing stage and his visits to the site were necessary to get a good finishing. The finishing touches to all walls and garden laying work were pending still.

Ashok had to relent and his parents left for Koduru next day in a bus as his dad did not want a car for the trip.

* * *

One evening, that was a Saturday, Ashok was free and was at home early. They were taking tea in the backyard garden and the baby was asleep in the bed room. The evening breeze was refreshing, with flower plants around passing mild fragrances. They were enjoying the tea while sitting in the garden chairs and low table.

Ashok said with a smile "Mala, the second factory too has picked up production now."

Mala smiling "That is a good-news. And you were giving jobs to those Koduru guys, how are they?"

"They are working alright. They have been given training and my brother-in-law is good at extracting work."

Mala said "Yes, he is an experienced executive."

Ashok "But now there is a hitch in running the businesses, two factories of new wood and my own first one."

Mala "Why? Everything is fixed now. Mr. Venkat is there as C.E.O. Do you need another C.E.O.?"

Ashok "Not that. I am there to work other matters. But it is about funds. With partnership and loan burden with periodic interest payment, we don't have sufficient funds. For construction of second go-down we had problems. We somehow finished it."

Mala "So, what is the solution?"

Ashok smiled and said "We have to take more partners for contributing funds, but there are restrictions on the number. So, the way out is to convert this in to a private limited company. Then we can go up to fifty members. Without taking loans, we can get funds as investments by new members. We can take some relatives or friends as new members."

Mala "That is good."

Ashok "I have to speak to Mohan and then to my brother-in-law about this,"

Mala smiled "O.K., go ahead. I fully concur with you."

* * *

After a week on a Sunday, Ashok called Mohan and said "I have been thinking about funds crunch. There are limits for our contributions or loans from banks. Loans are burdensome and not available readily too. So, I thought why not take more partners in to the group. But there are limits for partnership, as you know. So, the solution is making this a Limited Company."

Mohan at once said "I also thought that way. Converting these firms in to Private Limited Companies is best solution."

Ashok "So, we will sit with Mala and Ramya too and discuss about this. Can you come over with Ramya for discussion today?"

Mohan smiled "Dinner in your house is tempting. But I would also ask Ramya if she is free."

Ashok "Certainly, you please make a call."

* * *

By evening six, the visit was confirmed as Ramya did not have any appointments or urgent work. So Ramya agreed to go over to Mohan's place to spend time with Mala and baby.

They were with Ashok and family in the backyard garden afterwards. The baby not named yet but called 'Sree' accompanied them.

Mala called "Sree, come to me."

Sree did not move. She was not willing.

Ramya made her relent by telling her that if she goes to aunty Mala, she could take the baby of her in to her hands. The baby, not named yet but called 'Babu' was in the lap of his mother. Sree then went to Mala.

Coming to the subject for discussion, Mohan asked Ashok, "So, what are the plans for membership mobilization?"

Ashok said "I think the subject does not need introduction. Ramya may like to express her opinion."

Ramya "Yes, we must take more members. There cannot be any second opinion about that. Now who would like to join as new members?'

Mala "I talked to my father. He is willing Sagar to join this. And about the number of shares and investment amount, I don't know."

Ramya "That is fine. Sagar, your brother could become a member. That is within the family. My father-in-law is already a member."

Ashok said "We must have more members at least ten or fifteen to start with so that we can have sufficient capital. We can also think of friends."

Mohan "why not? Even reliable employees too could be taken as members."

Ramya "Yes. Why not?"

All of them laughed. Sree joined them assuming that to be a joke, while trying hold Babu in her hands. Ramya prevented any mishap by helping her.

Ramya said "Employee-relatives, say Mr. Venkat could be asked if he takes shares."

Mohan "Yes, Mr. Venkat has to be a member. Even as per our agreement we have to give him some shares. Of course, quantity not decided yet."

Mala "Sure, that means, he is already in."

Ashok "The shares could be ten thousand rupees each and depending on the intended investment, the number of shares would be worked out."

Mohan "For working out the details and formation of company we have to talk to our consultant Mr. Rajesh."

Ashok "Yes, Rajesh, we must talk to. Before that we must finalize the names of other members we propose to admit. Now we added names of Sagar and Venkat."

Ramya smiled and said "From my side, if it does not go against your principles, Mrs. Jaya, who helped me with the baby 'Sree' can be given a small number of shares."

Mala "Yes, certainly. She is like a family member to us."

Ashok "Yes, she is."

Ramya "I would pay for the shares allotted to her, whatever number it is."

Mohan "As Ramya said, if it does not go against our principles, manager of factory one could be given some shares."

Ashok smiled "My goodness, in fact we forgot about him. About principle, we are here to decide the principles. He must be given a chance and I will pay for his shares."

Mohan "Mr. Rajesh has been with us, since many years, can we offer him some shares?"

Ashok smiled "Yes, yes, that would be a good gesture. And the shares amount, he can bare, I think. He is a practicing consultant."

Mala said with a welcome smile "It is dinner time."

Ashok "It is dinner now. Later we will call and sit with Rajesh and Mr. Venkat, in the next meeting and make the details clear."

Mohan "Yes, dinner from the kitchen of Ashok and Mala with Mr. Nair in attendance is a great expectancy. My father-in-law wanted to snatch him away from here."

He laughed joined by others.

* * *

23

In the conference room of factory one, Ashok and Mohan sat with Rajesh, the consultant. They were discussing about the formation of the Limited Company.

Mr. Rajesh said "Mr. Ashok, now we are planning to convert the second factory as a Private Limited Company. The first one, The Perfect Wood Products, remains as a partnership firm, with you two as partners I suppose."

Ashok said "Yes Rajesh, that is right. In the second factory we will admit some more members. At present Mr. Mohan, Mr. Dasaradh, Mrs. Malathi and myself are partners in factory two. We had discussed and added Mr. Sagar s/o Mr. Narender, Mr. Venkat, C.E.O., Mrs. Jaya nominated by Mrs. Ramya, Mr. Ramesh, manager factory one and last but not least Mr. Rajesh, yourself."

Mr. Rajesh smiled and said "Sir, I am honoured and glad."

Mohan said "Yes, Mr. Rajesh, it is fair to include you, as our advisor and well-wisher."

Ashok smiled and said "Mohan, I forgot to add Dr. Varada, our technical consultant."

Mohan "Yes, without doubt he must be with us. And he has accepted to be with us."

Ashok "Next, we have to plan about the number of shares. We decided to make each share of one lakh rupees value. We thought share value could be ten thousand, but better to have higher value and less number, as it is a private limited company. And Mohan and I began the firm, with ten crores each that works out to one thousand shares each. Next Mr. Dasaradh and Mrs. Malathi five crores each already invested. So, the initial capital, already invested in the firm comes to thirty crores. Mr. Venkat and Sagar accepted for five hundred shares each. We fixed two hundred shares each to Mr. Rajesh and Dr. Varada. And finally fifty shares each to Mr. Ramesh and Mrs. Jaya, half of the amounts due from each are to be borne by us and the rest, they pay in instalments."

Mr. Rajesh "So, the total number of shares work out to four thousand and five hundred, at the rate of one lakh each share. So, total paid up capital becomes forty-five crores now."

Mohan "That's right Mr. Rajesh. We started the firm with eighty crores total capital, including loan."

Ashok "We already paid thirty crores as our share of investment."

Rajesh "Yes, Mr. Ashok, I have those figures and the project report with me."

Mohan "We can continue with that total capital figure, I think."

Rajesh "Yes, if we want, we can reduce the loan portion by repaying. I think it could be for building and machinery only as land is your own."

Ashok said "That's right, Mr. Rajesh."

Rajesh said "We can keep the authorised capital as one hundred crores. So, now that gives a clear picture of the company to be formed. Regarding the name, we have to decide."

Ashok said "We can change the name too as the new members are more than existing. The company too is not old enough to have high good-will. O.K., Mr. Rajesh."

Mohan "We can decide the name in the meeting of members."

Ashok "That's right. We will do that."

Rajesh "O.K., Mr. Mohan. I will inform date of our next meeting after finishing formalities, Mr. Ashok."

The meeting came to an end, with coffees.

* * *

Mr. Rajesh called for a meeting of all the proposed members of the company to be formed to formally introduce to the details and also to one another.

They assembled at the conference room of the factory one, named The Perfect Wood Products.

Mr. Rajesh welcomed the assembled people and explained the details of the share capital and the shares allotted to each member as informed by the main partners of the firm, now to be converted in to a private limited company.

He read out the names and shares—

"The members proposed and the shares for each at one lakh rupees per share, proposed to be allotted to them are as follows.

Mr. Ashok and Mr. Mohan one thousand shares each.

Mr. Dasaradh and Mrs. Malathi five hundred shares each.

Mr. Venkat and Mr. Sagar five hundred shares each.

Mr. Rajesh and Mr. Varada two hundred shares each.

Mrs. Jaya and Mr. Ramesh fifty shares each

Total number of shares work out to four thousand five hundred and the amount comes to forty-five crores rupees.

Now we have to choose a name for the company.

Mr. Ashok and Mr. Mohan have you decided about the name for the company?"

Ashok said "I request any of the members to suggest a name, and we will go by majority opinion.

He smiled.

Mohan said "Ladies are good at selecting names.

Ramya who attended the meeting on invitation, though not a member said" Yes, that's right. Mala is an artist and she must be good in creative ideas."

Mohan "Yes, I came to know that Mala painted many good pictures. In fact, Ramya proposed a solo exhibition of her paintings some time in future in Vizag."

Mala smiled and said "Please give me a few minutes to think and in the meantime, Mr. Rajesh could proceed with other items in the agenda."

Mr. Rajesh "O.K., madam. Now I will proceed with the details required for registration, say, the election of chairman and managing director."

Ashok said "Mohan will be the managing director and Mr. Dasaradh will be the Chairman."

Rajesh "That's fine and any other names suggested by others?"

Mala said "That is fine sir. We all accept the names."

Venkat "That's good. We all accept the proposal."

Mohan "If that is so, Ashok could be the joint M.D. In my absence he must take care of the affairs of the company as we share our responsibilities now."

Ashok "O.K. No problem."

All clapped and shouted 'Yes' in unison.

Rajesh said addressing Mala "Madam, can you suggest the name now?

Mala said with a smile "I suggest the name as 'Premium Wood Company Limited'."

All the members clapped in unison accepting the name.

Rajesh said "O.K. I will note down that."

He again said "With that we come to the conclusion. And we will meet again after the formation of the company. Congratulations to all."

Ashok and Mohan said in unison "Thank you, Mr. Rajesh."

Others followed them.

Then they all had tea and snacks with hearty exchanges of greetings on the formation of the company.

* * *

24

Ramya and Mohan planned a solo exhibition of paintings of Mala.

Ramya told Mohan after they went home from the company meeting "Mohan, I saw Mala's paintings in their house. They are exceptional. Very original way of painting. I had been following the art exhibitions of some modern artists. I don't think she lags them behind in any way. So, I thought why not we put them in an exhibition for public so they too can share the joy of watching good paintings."

Mohan "Yes, Ramya, that's a good idea I was not knowing that Mala was such a good artist. My uncle used to say, that Mala paints occasionally. That was whenever she found time. That happened during her holidays, I think."

Ramya smiled and said "It's odd. Your cousin's paintings you have not seen till now."

Mohan "No, no, I saw some paintings in their house. But I did not ask them about the artist. That may be because I am not an art lover."

Ramya "Now, we will take this opportunity of putting them for public view. We must get a hall for that."

Mohan "I know someone in the university administration. I will ask him to provide one of the halls available for meetings. This is for one day or more?"

Ramya "May be for two days or more. If the word spreads more people would like to watch the paintings."

Mohan "We will give an advertisement or we inform the newspaper people? They have a column for the cultural programs."

Ramya "Yes, that's right."

Mohan "I will talk to that university man. Did you talk to Mala, about this?"

Ramya smiled and said "No, I will talk to her today. And you have to find the dates of availability of the hall. I think we have to gather the paintings, may be some of them from Mala's house at Rajolu."

Mohan "No problem, I will bring them and also I will invite my uncle and aunt for their daughter's painting exhibition."

Ramya "Thank you. We have work to do now. I will contact newspaper people."

Mohan "O.K., then."

* * *

There was a banner at a distance in front of the hall over the pathway leading to the hall. The administrative office had put up a board indicating about the exhibition. Both read 'Mrs. Malathi's painting exhibition on 25th and 26th of October 2018."

At evening six thirty, many from the university staff quarters, made a beeline to the hall. The exhibition was put up right in their campus. So, who would miss the opportunity? The womenfolk with children arrived there in groups.

They have kept a coffee, tea and snacks stall. They came from the university canteen.

After that first group, visitors from the city started flowing in. They had plenty of parking place too.

Ashok and Mala and Ramya and Mohan were at the entrance, standing near the statue of one of the founders of the university. Mala's parents, Mr. Narender and his wife were beside them.

After some time, some visitors with artistic insight began discussing amongst themselves, standing in front of one of the exhibits. Mala and Ramya went to them and Ramya introduced the artist to them. When they put questions to her Mala answered them to their satisfaction.

In all, there were eighteen exhibits. Some were landscapes, and others still-pictures. There were no portraits as she did not evince interest in them. She told them so. Some visitors wanted to know the prices, the manager of the hall told them that they were not for sale, as informed by the artist.

It went on up to nine thirty and then the visitors thinned out. The press persons from two dailies, interviewed Mala for a few minutes and took photographs.

Mala thanked Ramya and Mohan for their effort in organising the exhibition.

Ashok and Mala invited Mohan and Ramya for dinner to their house after closure of the exhibition. Mala's parents too thanked Ramya and Mohan for making the exhibition a possibility.

* * *

They enjoyed the eight-course dinner with pleasant exchanges and anecdotes. They then shifted to the garden in the backyard. Nair ordered for special betel rolls for them. The occasion was special as Malathi became a celebrated artist known around the city and going to be more, by the time the newspapers were out on the stands.

The children Sree and Babu were left in the care of the maid and playing inside.

Ramya said "I am glad I could succeed in getting the assent of Mala for this exhibition and could fix it with the cooperation of Mohan."

Ashok said "Yes, Ramya, we are thankful to you both for all the trouble you had taken."

Ramya "That's O.K., Ashok. Next thing is how to help Mala to continue with her painting work. Mala, are you busy with the company work still?"

Ashok "I don't think so. I am attending to that, as she has to take care of Babu."

Mohan "Ashok, why don't you fix a manager for your factory?"

Ashok "Yes, I think I must do that now. The supply to Defence departments is now regularised. And there are no chances for any new market. Moreover Power wood business is new and expanding. I must be concentrating more on this now. So, I must think of fixing a manager for my old business. Even if he is a retired person it is O.K."

Mohan "That's right. Mala can be free then for painting."

Ramya smiling said "And where will she be painting in this bungalow? Any room you thought for that?"

Ashok "I think, for her to be comfortable, is the southern bedroom in the first floor. She can have a good view of the garden below. I will get that room cleared for her."

Mala smiled "My goodness, with all this attention, I feel embarrassed. And I must think about the way to do some really good work now. I have greater responsibility now."

Mr. Narender, Mala's father said, "Yes, my child, you can engage yourself in your favourite hobby freely. I am glad they are so considerate to you."

Ramya "My best wishes to you, Mala."

They all laughed cheerfully.

* * *

25

Mr. Krishnarao called Ashok and said "Ashok, my son, the building work is completed. The electrification and plumbing work are also finished now. You can plan to come here one day and see for yourself. If anything is not right or if you need changes, you can point out that to the contractor. This must be done before he is paid. I think you have to fix the payments to contractors too."

Ashok said "O.K. dad, on Saturday, we can come and Sunday evening we will be back here. Mala and Babu are fine."

* * *

Mala began her painting activity in the upstairs bedroom, now modified in to an art studio.

The room was furnished with two racks and a few painting-stands. She began painting the picture of the garden in the backyard on a medium sized canvas. Ashok suggested to her to take a few snaps of the place in advance, so that she could avoid sitting there and drawing sketches. But she declined and said making sketches was half the painting work done because thinking about the subject has been decided in advance.

Ashok said "Yes, may be so. I agree I am a novice as far as art work is concerned.'

He laughed away.

* * *

On Saturday, they started early by seven in the morning, Babu was given food and readied by the maid. Ashok and Mala had breakfast by then. Ashok informed Mohan about their trip to Koduru.

The driver was ready by six thirty. They wanted to reach Koduru early, so that the hot weather would not be a problem for the baby.

As they had called his father before starting, his mother and father were waiting in the front room. As soon as they reached their house, Ashok's mother took the baby in her arms and they walked in.

As that was second Saturday, it was a holiday for Subbu, his cousin. Subbu came with his daughter there after some time, to say hello to them. And his daughter wanted to play with the baby. Mala and her mother-in-law began chatting about Vizag and all the matters connected to their families.

After some time Subbu left them with his daughter.

Ashok and his father went to the construction site of the building. The contractor was there supervising some workers near the compound wall.

The compound wall was finished but the gate was not fixed. The wall was yet to be painted with distemper.

The building looked grand with the biscuit colour outdoor paint finished on it. As they entered the hall next to the portico, there were two rooms on either side. The broad portico in the front gave a good frontal view. There was another larger hall behind the first one with a staircase at one end to reach the first floor. Next to this hall a kitchen and dining hall, finished the ground floor picture. Then, they went up the steps to the first floor and reached the hall. Next to the hall, there were three bedrooms with entrances in to the hall. In front of the hall a large area was left to the sky, with parapet wall around, to provide a sit out for a few dozens of visitors at a time.

Except for some suggestions about the balustrade and the front windows in the hall on the ground floor, Ashok felt satisfied with the work. The contractor had followed them to the first floor and Ashok told him about the changes to be made. The contractor assented. He told them that the compound wall would be painted in a fast colour. Ashok wanted it to be either scarlet colour or light blue. Ashok paid the contractor in cheque, a part payment. As the final paymentwould be made after two weeks to check any lapses or corrections in construction and finishing.

Ashok and his father reached home by lunch time.

* * *

26

It was nine in the late evening. Ramya and Mohan sat in easy chairs playing with Sree on the terrace of their home. The moon was shining in the sky with pleasant light all around. The southern winds swayed the coconut trees down below, with leaves shining in the moon light.

Sree, four years old now, asked her mother, "Mom, how is that the moon stays there without any support?"

Ramya looked in to the face of Mohan with a smile, for his comment. Mohan became thoughtful.

Ramya told Sree "I don't know if I could answer that to make you understand."

Mohan got an answer in the meantime and said "Baby dear, moon does not stay there. It makes rounds around earth, on which we are now. That is like airplane travelling on sky, but moon moves slower than airplane."

Sree said laughing "Yes, it moves slowly. But it carries whom?"

Mohan became silent.

Ramya picked up the conversation and said "It won't carry any body. It is so small, you see, it carries only light for us all."

Mohan smiled "Well explained in an intelligent way."

Sree "Yes, it carries light for us till morning. I know."

Ramya "Exactly, so."

Ramya said "Now we go for sleep, O.K."

She tried to get up.

Sree pleaded," Mom, tell me a story."

Ramya "Wait, wait, O.K., I will tell you a story."

She thought over for a few moments and began "When I was a small child, we were at the railway station at Vijayawada. You know railway station?"

Sree "Yes, I know, I saw Waltair station."

Ramya "O.k. we will continue. Myself and my mom were there on the platform. We were waiting for our train to Vizag. We sat on a bench. After sometime, I observed a cockroach emerging from a crevice under the bench, where we sat. It was slowly moving towards the edge of platform."

Sree "Yes".

Ramya "It was trying to go towards the rail line, where odd things thrown by passengers lie. But due to the sound of footsteps of passengers, it returned to where we sat. It happened many times."

Sree "Yes, but it might get crushed under some one's feet."

Ramya "Exactly, that was why it returned. And I too was afraid of that possibility and was shouting and cautioning passengers passing by, about the cockroach. Luckily it escaped many times."

Ramya continued and the baby was listening attentively to the story, even without batting an eyelid.

"Then it was announced that our train was arriving on the platform. All started getting up and moving. I and my mom too picked up our bags and got up and proceeded to our coach hurriedly. At that time, I felt something crushed under my foot. My God, when I looked down, I saw the cockroach which I was trying to save got crushed right under my foot and dead. I felt very bad."

Sree shouted with anguish "What mom, you crushed it dead. You should have seen it."

She began crying.

Mohan and Ramya told her "That was only a story, don't cry, baby."

They laughed. And Mohan carried the baby towards the bedroom, followed by Ramya.

* * *

Mohan was in the midst of taking his breakfast and his phone rang. It was his father.

He enquired about the baby.

Mohan said "Dad, Sree is fine and she is very inquisitive. Yesterday, in the evening we were sitting in the open place on the second floor. She saw the moon and she began putting so many questions about moon, we could not answer them. She asked how the moon was hanging in the sky without any support."

His father laughed aloud "Children in that age would be like that only. That's good for her. Another topic now, do you remember I suggested some time back that we should have a family-get-together? Now everything is settled and all are in good moods. You can plan for one now."

Mohan said with a smile "Yes, Dad, I will do that. I will talk to my partner, Ashok too. He has become a family member to us now."

His dad said "O.K., that's right, as you please."

* * *

Mohan finished his breakfast and at once called Ashok.

"Hi, Ashok, are you free?"

"Yes, Mohan."

"Ashok, do you remember my dad suggested, long back, we should have a family get together. He made a call now enquiring about Sree. Then he suddenly remembered about that get together."

"Yes, I remember that day. It was the day when we performed ground breaking ceremony for the factory. I talked to Mala about meeting frequently being residents of Vizag and so on. A few days later, I proposed to Mala and she assented."

He laughed loudly and Mohan joined him.

Mohan "After that day, so many incidents happened in our families. But I forgot about that get together till now."

"Yes, Mohan. We have come a long way now after that."

"Now that, we are good in business too, it is time we celebrate the present happy days."

"Yes, Mohan, you plan for family meet. But is it for family only or staff are also part of it?"

"What is your opinion? It is good to include staff and their families too, I think."

"Yes, but instead of ourselves deciding that, we will talk to our wives and other family members too."

Mohan "Then, why not we have a meeting of our family members in advance?"

Ashok "Yes, that is a better idea. We will meet and decide. You fix a day for all our family members to meet."

"I will call my dad and uncle, that is Mala's father. You too call your parents. Ramya's parents also we can call, I think."

Ashok "We will include them certainly."

Mohan "Mr. Venkat is a family member and also a staff member. So, it is fair to include staff members too, when Mr. Venkat is one of them. I think this situation in fact settled the matter. Any way we will call for a meeting of our family members."

Ashok "What you said is right. Because of my brother-in-law, the matter has a ready solution now. Any way, we will meet with all family members first. They too will get the satisfaction of taking part in the decision taking. And that too for a family get together party. That, family members coming together happened, long back, I think."

Mohan "Yes, Ashok, that's right. We will all meet."

* * *

Mohan called his dad and asked him about the inclusion of staff and their families in the get together and also to come to the meeting to decide that.

Dasaradh said "Mohan, I will not be able to come to the meeting to decide that. You, Ashok and others decide. Either way it's o.k. for us. You can call your uncle Narender too."

Mohan then called Narender and he said that he would be able to come by weekend, as they wanted to spend time with Mala and grandson.

Mohan passed on the information to Ashok. Ashok then called his father-in-law Mr. Narender and called them to come over for weekend. He told Venkat and sister Bala about the meeting.

Ashok told Neelima and Shyam about the get together. Then he called Sagar too to inform him, though already he told his father.

So, finally that weekend was fixed for the preliminary meeting.

Ashok said they would all meet at his house for dinner as Nair would be there for arranging the meals.

* * *

On Saturday, in the evening, they all met in the garden at the back of Ashok's bungalow.

Mala said "It's fair to call the staff also once in a while and their family members must also participate."

Ramya "I agree with Mala on that. That is a kind of motivation for the staff. Even if you give bonus every year, this kind of personal approach matters much."

Bala "I would vote with Ramya and Mala. We are part of the staff and also family."

She laughed and others joined her.

Malathi's father Narender agreed with Mala and Ramya too.

Maruthirao, father of Ramya said "It's a small matter. If the expenditure is considered, it is negligible. And the question of status, such a get together with staff and their families enhances our status. It will not lessen our status by any means."

Venkat was simply smiling, because he did not want to express anything more than what his wife Bala said.

Krishnarao, father of Ashok too agreed for participation of the staff and their families.

After chitchat for two hours, they attended dinner in the hall, prepared under the supervision of Nair.

It was a buffet dinner so that each can meet others and converse freely.

Mohan and Ashok felt happy and they knew the concurrence of opinions even before the meeting.

The get together of family and staff was planned to be on a festival day or weekend.

* * *

The family get together finally happened on the Saturday of subsequent week. The venue was a function hall in Visakha Restaurant.

Neelima and her husband Shyam attended the get together, after a number of persistent calls by her father and Mala. They came from Pune for two days stay, as Shyam could not get leave for more days.

Parents of Ramya too attended the function.

All the staff members including Bhaskar, husband of Jaya, attended. Some of the staff members were from Koduru, that included Dinakar and also the son of Sunder who joined the company by then.

Consultants Dr. Varada and Rajesh took part in the gathering with their families.

The get together started at four in the evening, with the families of staff and those of promoters, familiarising with each other, in a slow and enthusiastic approach. The entire gathering was in smiles of exuberance and joy as it was a rare occasion.

Around two dozen family members from each group, of staff and promoters attended the function. There were snacks and cool drinks and coffee and tea for those who needed them.

There was a dinner afterwards.

The evening turned out to be more pleasant than expected by either group.

Promoters' family members offered special thanks to Mr. Dasaradh, father of Mohan, for his persistent desire for conducting such a function, which ended in such a success.

* * *

27

Ramya called Mala,

"Hi, Malathi, how is the painting activity going on?"

Mala smiled and said "Fine, Thank you, Ramya. I have done one painting of my garden in the backyard. I have to do the finishing touches to that."

"That's good. What is the next project?"

"Really so, it's a project only. At first, I have to make a sketch on the drawing paper and transfer that to the canvas as truthfully as possible. Then painting part, make and remake the work. It's really a project."

"Yes, yes, I understand. It is a tedious job. Taj Mahal must have been a tedious job for those architects and craftsmen. But once finished it's a 'joy for ever' to look at."

"Right, quite right, it is done with utmost concentration and dedication. May be any art work, or even story writing too, is like that."

"Yes, I tell stories, bed time ones, to 'Sree'. I just weave stories as the situation comes up, not difficult though."

"Yes, even in the case of painting too, artist doesn't feel it tedious. Whether painting or storytelling, it is a pleasure to the artist, but it might appear tedious to observers. Now, coming to the subject of stories, why don't you write them down?"

"I never thought I could do that. With your encouraging words, I may try to do that hereafter."

Ramya continued "Mala, I made this call actually to remind you about the function of naming the children, you for Babu and I for Sree."

Mala said "My goodness, I forgot about that altogether. Time moves on without our effort and things get postponed before we know it."

Ramya "So, I will talk to Mohan to speak to Ashok too and fix up a place and date for that."

Mala "O.K., Ramya, that's good. Please talk to him. I too would tell Ashok about this."

Ramya "Bye, Malathi."

Mala "Bye, Ramya."

* * *

Mohan and Ashok met in the conference room of the company and discussed about performing the naming ceremony of their children.

Mohan said "We will hire a function hall that is large and centrally located."

Ashok said "As we planned, it must accommodate a few hundred invitees. All the staff members and their families would be present, as this is our first function after the formation of the company. They would certainly expect a grand reception, that too for a common function of two directors together at one place."

Mohan "Added to that, our customers, dealers and users, whom we must invite. It is a good gesture and also a kind of propagation of the product."

Mohan "In business families whatever you do has two edges even if you don't mean it."

Ashok smiled and said "We will make it memorable after all these years of struggle for the business by staff members and users and dealers and last but not least ourselves."

He added "I will check for a large and centrally located function hall and its availability on the days fixed by our *pundits*."

Mohan "Yes, Ashok, but, for these arrangements we can take the help of manager Mr. Ramesh and new manager of your factory, Mr. Shyam Prasad, too. Have you told your brother-in-law about the function?"

Ashok said "Yes, I have already informed him. He felt happy about the naming ceremony."

* * *

Mr. Ramesh had a relative in the office of Omkar function hall. It was large and located near the railway station. He could get the function hall booked for one day on twentieth of January, the day fixed by *pandits* for the naming ceremony.

Ramya and Mala made a draft invitation card with a provision for printing each invitation on the insides of the twofold card. The print would be in Telugu and time, date and place of function would be in English too, so that those who do not know Telugu language could follow the details of the function.

When the cards were ready, they were distributed to the relatives of Ashok and Mohan. The responsibility for distributing the cards among staff and dealers and customer companies was given to Ramesh and Shyam Prasad, managers.

Ashok took care to send the invitations to the residents of Koduru, where he had childhood contacts. He wanted make bridges with the past connections and make them amiable towards him.

Mohan's parents reached his home two days before the function. His sister and brother-in-law spoke to him and to Mr. Dasaradh, expressing their inability to come due to their preoccupation with some urgent work of house repair. Mohan's sister spoke to Ramya too and expressed her regrets for their absence in spite of their extreme desire to attend the function. Ashok's parents and Subbu's family came down to Ashok's house a day before the function.

The hall was decorated all around with abundant flowers and mango leaves. At the time fixed by the priests for the ceremony, Ashok and Mala and Mohan and Ramya were seated on the dais of the hall with each of their children sitting in front of them. The *purohits* sat opposite to each couple and began arranging the *pooja* materials in an order. The coconuts, flowers, turmeric laced rice, betel leaves and so on were in front of them. Pictures of deities were kept there.

The invitees were entering the hall in groups after their breakfast in the dining hall situated next to the function hall on the right side. The number of invitees rose to around a couple hundreds and more.

Ashok's sister and mother sat close him and Mala. And Mohan's mother sat next to him and Ramya.

The first row before the dais was occupied by the close relatives of both the couples, performing the ceremony. Representatives of the dealers and construction companies sat after the relatives. Staff members and the invited Koduru residents sat in their respective groups. They were all busy in chatting among them.

The ceremony began with the chanting of *Vedic mantras* by the *purohits*. All the murmuring sounds of the invitees stopped now and they began paying attention to the ceremony.

After an hour of the routine of the ceremony, the *purohits* made the parents of each child write the names of each one on the rice spread in a large silver plates in front of them. Then the *purohits* sprinkled turmeric rice as blessings, on the people sitting on the dais, starting with each child and their parents.

All the relatives were asked to sprinkle the turmeric rice on each child now given name.

As the ceremony had come to a conclusion there was relaxation all around the hall. Each group of invitees began their chatting and pleasantries among themselves.

Then they all were asked to take lunch in the dining hall.

Ashok and Mohan paid special attention to Mr. Kashyap, the President of the All India Dealers Association. They led him to the dining hall while speaking about business and other things.

Mr. Kashyap, a man of pleasant disposition, in his fifties was free in conversation with the Directors. They sat with the served lunch plates in hands, at one corner of the hall near the cool ambience of a Neem tree.

Mr. Kashyap said with a broad smile, while munching spoon-fulls of biryani "Mr. Ashok, I am really glad to be among so many people committed to the production and distribution of Power Wood."

Mohan interrupted with a smile "Mr. Kashyap, there are users also, representatives from the construction companies."

Mr. Kashyap "I see. There are some people who appear like farmers from village, are they so?"

Ashok said with a laughter "They are from my native place, Koduru. Some of them are my class mates in school and friends."

Mr. Kashyap while eating a savoury said "My goodness, you have called all those with whom you played with, in childhood."

Ashok "Yes, yes, I have to call them to share the happy occasion with me."

Mohan excused and left on a call from his dad.

Kashyap said "That's great. In fact, I have to emulate you in this. That is a good gesture."

Ashok came closer to Kashyap and said "My dear sir, I was not like this before. I changed my attitude after some realization."

Kashyap said "Please tell me. I am observing you and Mr. Mohan keeping such a good relationship with all your town people. I am in a kind of dilemma to deal with the interruptions of childhood guys in my personal affairs, whom you cannot despatch altogether."

Ashok said "I was in the same situation, some time back. But I understood by experience that we cannot avoid childhood contacts. In case you want to avoid, you will have to pay the price by worrisome days. It is difficult to keep them in bad mood throughout, without spoiling your health. So, I changed myself for my good and started keeping good relationship with whoever approaching me. Now I am happy and people say I have become radiant in my appearance."

He laughed loudly.

Kashyap joined him.

Kashyap said "My goodness. I know now why you are appearing so welcome guy. I now realize that I did a good thing to come here and have a personal talk with you."

He continued "In fact, I had a family function to attend. My sister's daughter's birthday happens to be today. I avoided attending that to fulfil a business commitment. I have no regrets now."

Ashok smiled and said "Thank you, Mr. Kashyap, for your appreciation."

Subbu came there to tell Ashok that he was leaving for his place as some urgent work was there for him.

Ashok got up and talked with him for some time and then Subbu left.

Mr. Kashyap took betel roll and began munching on that enjoying the flavour. He then shook hands with Ashok and left the place.

* * *

28

Kashyap while coming out, saw Ramesh at one corner of the function hall, near the dining place. He was surprised to see him there.

He said "Why? Ramesh! You are here? What are you doing here?"

Ramesh too was surprised and said "Kashyap sir, when did you come here?"

Kashyap smiling "I am connected to this business. I am President of the Dealers Association."

He continued "But what are you doing here?"

"I am working as a manager in the factory here sir. I know you are in the invitee's list. But I did not expect you sir, being such a busy man."

"I see. You left us and appeared here suddenly."

"Where are you put up sir?"

Kashyap thought for a while and said "I am in Ramakrishna Hotel. I want to talk to you. You come to my room 403. But you must see me before nine. I am leaving tonight."

He gave his card.

Ramesh said "Yes, sir, I will see you there."

Kashyap was gone.

Shyam Prasad, manager of Ashok's factory, who was standing at a distance came to Ramesh now and asked Ramesh "Who is that man?"

Ramesh replied "I worked for his business at Delhi for a decade. They have big hardware and wood dealership and also many other business dealings."

* * *

Ramesh reached Ramakrishna Hotel near the beach. The hotel faced the sea and situated at a distance of a kilometre from sea.

Ramesh showed the visiting card given by Kashyap to the watchman there. He went inside and the manager sent a boy to escort him to the room of Kashyap. When Kashyap accepted him, the boy was gone. Kashyap smiled to Ramesh and led him to the balcony at the back. He did not want anyone to hear their conversation.

Kashyap asked Ramesh.

"Tell me Ramesh, how is life here?"

"Fine sir, they pay well and many known persons of me are here. Life is good. The company offered me some shares too as a kind of bonus, sir."

"That's good, you are settled here after coming away from Delhi. But, still I want you to come back to Delhi again and guide me in this business of Power Wood."

"I have to think over, sir."

Ramesh smiled with embarrassment, for being given so much importance.

Kashyap "Don't think for a moment that I will not pay you better than them."

He continued "Now, coming to the point, I want to start making those power wood panels near home and supply to many aspirant users there."

"But sir, Ashok sir has the 'lease for long term' for that formula."

Ramesh "That's O.K., but, still we will approach the original Patent holder and bargain for a lease for production in the north."

"O.K., sir,"

"We will do that, Ramesh. You do me the favour of sending me the details of the name and address of the original patent holder, I know it is a research organisation. You also send me the address of the machine maker who supplied the machinery."

"O.K., sir."

Kashyap "You slowly withdraw from that company of Ashok and join us. I will make you the director of the new company making the Power Wood."

He then pulled out his cheque book and wrote a cheque for some amount beyond the expectation of Ramesh.

He gave the cheque to Ramesh.

Ramesh at first refused but accepted on Kashyap's insistence.

"We want to go ahead with the production of Permanent Wood, that's what I call that now. You send me the details at the earliest and try getting away from this company and reach Delhi as early as possible. Much depends on your cooperation too."

Kashyap rose from his seat.

Ramesh got up and paid respects to Kashyap.

Kashyap patted him on the back.

Ramesh left him then, with the cheque in pocket and a smile on his face.

* * *

By next day Kashyap was in Delhi.

He received the information, he wanted from Ramesh.

He called the Research Institute which had the original patent. They informed him about the Premium Wood Company of Ashok and Mohan and said they could not help him at that time as the lease was already in force.

He then called the machinery supplier company and they asked him to send some representative for discussion. He thought over the matter. He knew they would ask for documents of lease and so on. It was a confidential matter and he would have to convince them about the safety of the deal which was out of the way business. So, he planned to visit Nagpur himself and meet them personally. He made adjustment in his schedule, and then proceeded to Nagpur. He checked for the address and reached the premises of the company. It was a small company manufacturing machinery on orders. They make and assemble machinery for wood laminations and also any other machinery, if the design and purpose were specified. It had a name board with the name 'Digvijay Machinery Manufacturers'. Kashyap was led to the office room by the receptionist.

The C.E.O. an old man Mr. Digvijay received Kashyap in his office room with a broad smile.

Mr. Digvijay said "But sir, we supply this machinery only on producing the lease documents as the Research Organisation is a Semi Government unit and the process is confidential."

Kashyap said "Sir, you tell me the way out, as we are getting enquiries for such wood panels at Delhi."

Mr. Digvijay said "I know, I know sir, the material is popular in the South already. It has been replacing cement and bricks for walls. In fact, cement company lobbies are concerned about this development."

Kashyap said "Yes, they may lose some business due to this. The concern is genuine. But the process is approved by the Government."

Digvijay "Yes, that's right. And you know Mr. Ashok could get all the required permissions from government for the production of these wood panels. They named it Power Wood."

Kashyap coming back to his query, asked "So, you tell me, what is the solution?"

Digvijay "You have to be careful. If you want to make this in the north, you must make it at a remote place of a remote district.

Kashyap "I know, I will take care of that. We only supply to local users and construction firms, but not dealers."

Digvijay "You should not advertise and the matter should not come to the notice of officials. I am telling all this because, we are in the picture too."

Kashyap 'I know, we take care. We are in business since a few decades. We know how to deal with the officials."

Digvijay 'It is risky. Please take care and don't reveal us. On this condition, we supply and assemble the machinery for the Power Wood."

Kashyap smiled and said "We will call it Permanent Wood, not Power Wood, sir."

Digvijay too smiled "You name the firm also by some other name, not wood company, say furniture makers or some such name."

Kashyap "O.K. Then I am ready to pay advance now and please give me the schedule."

Digvijay "But, are you ready with the building?"

Kashyap "No building, we will make temporary sheds and install machinery in that,"

Digvijay "Whatever you like. But the payment will be at special rates."

Kashyap "O.K., agreed."

* * *

29

At Visakhapatnam, the effect of Kashyap's dealings had a mark on Premium Products Ltd. One day, after a week of his meeting with Kashyap, Ramesh told Ashok that he had personal problems and wanted to leave Vizag.

Ashok asked him with surprise "But how will you manage your family?"

Ramesh "My brother is at Delhi and my parents are with him. He asked me to come over there with family. He said he will take care of my employment there. He is having contacts with political people there."

Ashok said "O.K., of course I am surprised and not happy with this development. But I have no business to stop you. You must have thought of the consequences already and prepared. But I only urge you if possible, you please reconsider your decision."

He continued "Will you continue for two or three months till things could be handed over to someone else?"

Ramesh "I have to leave within a month sir."

Ashok "That becomes difficult for me. Can you continue till someone takes over?"

"After a month, I would like to be relieved sir, may be a week this side or that."

"O.K., Mr. Ramesh, you give me a letter to that effect. I will have to find a suitable person."

Ramesh left to his office room.

Ashok called Mohan and told him about the development.

Mohan asked him with surprise in his voice "How will you manage his absence?"

Ashok "I don't know. Just now he came and told me."

Mohan "We cannot get someone at once."

After a while Ashok said "I will talk to my brother-in-law, if he could help us till a new incumbent joins us."

Mohan "O.K., that is the only solution. The work is important one too. But why he wants to leave us so suddenly? Did you offer him increase in salary?"

Ashok "No. I did not. But you can call him and offer now. If he is ready, we can retain him for six months or so at least, so that we can make the new person familiarised with the work."

Mohan "Fine, I will try that."

* * *

Ashok was in his office at The Perfect Wood Products. The phone rang.

It was Dinakar of Koduru who was working at Premium Wood Products Ltd now.

Ashok said "Yes, Dinakar, what is the matter? Are you fine?"

Dinakar said "Yes, sir, I am fine. I wanted to tell you some information. That may be useful, I thought."

"O.K., tell me, what is it?"

"Sir, I came to know Ramesh wants to leave the company."

"Yes, he has some important work at Delhi."

Dinakar said "Sir, on the day of 'naming ceremony' I saw one Mr. Kashyap talking to Ramesh. When I asked him, who it was, he said he had worked with him at Delhi."

Ashok said "I see. He might be going back to Kashyap?"

"Yes, sir. I think so."

"O.K., Dinakar, thank you. Any way, he can go anywhere. Once he quits us, it does not matter."

"Please don't tell him sir that I told you about this."

Ashok smiled "No, problem on that, O.K."

* * *

Mohan came to Ashok after making a call. They sat in the office room.

"Yes, Mohan, any news?"

"Yes, I talked to Ramesh. He was not after money. He said he must go to his brother. That too he said urgently."

"O.K., just now Dinakar came here. He works in Premiun Ltd. He told me that Kashyap when he was here for the naming function, talked to Ramesh. They know each other."

"Mr. Kashyap of Delhi?"

"Yes, Dinakar told me that he worked with Mr. Kashyap at Delhi some years back. I don't know, he might be going to him. But why so urgently and to Kahsyap?"

Mohan "We cannot ask him. Let him go."

"This man Ramesh is not that knowledgeable or important that Kashyap wants him there."

"How he will be useful to him we don't know."

Mohan continued "I am thinking of putting a known person in the place of Ramesh. Bhaskar husband of Jaya is the man, I am thinking of. He is at present working with my father-in-law's company. But I can ask my father-in-law for lending him, till someone takes over. We can make use of him."

Ashok "O.K., Jaya's husband is a good choice. He is dependable and experienced too."

Mohan" If my father-in-law accepts, I will ask him and you can fix emoluments and other things. I will first find out if he is agreeable to this. Then I will send him to you."

Ashok "O.K., Mohan. That is a good arrangement, if he accepts. Otherwise we can offer better emoluments. And you may talk to Ramya too. She could put in a word to Jaya."

Ashok continued with a smile "Through proper channel, you know. Generally, nobody would like a change, unless it is beneficial or forced upon."

Mohan smiled "No, problem, I will do that."

Ashok "Yes, it is necessary. He is known in the family circles. Instead of getting a new person, he is certainly better. A good replacement."

Mohan "Yes, it is good replacement."

* * *

Mr. Krishnarao called Ashok and told him, it was time they conducted the *Grihapraveshan*, house warming function, of their new building, at Koduru. The building was complete in all respects. Ashok agreed and asked his dad to consult the *purohit* for an auspicious day for that. He said as soon as the date was fixed, he would come over there with his family and also bring the family of his sister Bala's family too. He said he would ask Mohan to attend the function. He said as it was a family-function, others need not be called.

Accordingly Mr. Krishnarao contacted his family *purohit* and they fixed January 20th for the performance of the function. He informed Ashok and Bala about that. Mr. Krishnarao invited his brother Narasimharao and his son Subbu with their family. Next he invited Mr. Narender father of Mala and Mr. Dasaradh father of Mohan with their families to attend the function. He then talked to his son in law, Venkat and invited them.

Ashok told his father that he would call some known persons of Koduru too for the function. Ashok also asked parents of Ramya to attend the function of house warming at Koduru.

* * *

Ashok arrived at Koduru with his family one day before. He had to help his father in the arrangements. His sister Bala and her family came in the evening of the same day, as Venkat had work to attend to.

Purohit was already arranged. They had called the caterer to supply morning breakfast and afternoon lunch for the guests. The watchman at the building attended to the decoration work. He fixed garlands of mango leaves with flowers at the main doorway and mango leaves at all door tops.

They had informed the function-material supplier about the *shamiana* for place of function and the dining place. They would also provide the furniture required for these activities.

The guests began arriving in the morning before the function time. They were taken to the breakfast tables.

At the *muhurat* time, Mr. Krishnarao and his wife sat for performing the ceremony and *homam* with *purohit* uttering the *mantras*. After the *pooja* the *purohit* led them to the main door with the utensil filled with sanctified water and they began sprinkling it in all the rooms. They were asked to break the coconuts at all doors and a pumpkin at the main door. The *purohit* then led them to the upstairs rooms and the procedure was repeated. The cow with the calf came later and was led through the doorways of all rooms of ground floor for sanctifying the place.

After completion of the rituals and offering of gifts, the guests were urged to go to the lunch enclosure. They were served lunch, on pre-arranged tables with cloth covers and the food was served on fresh banana leaves. The food items, in number of courses were served to the guests.

As the ceremony was performed by his mother and father, Ashok and Mala were free to take care of the guests. Mohan arrived at the time of the ceremony in the morning with his family. His father and mother came in advance. Mala's parents and brother came in time for the ceremony.

Ashok's old friends and locals were present too.

By three o' clock the guests began leaving the place, one family after the other. Only Mohan and Venkat's families remained.

Mohan asked Ashok "Now that function is over, what are the plans for using the house?"

Ashok looked at his father.

Mr. Krishnarao said "I have not thought of that yet. Ashok's mother says, we could move in to the new house. But we will become lonely here, as the town we lived, is at a distance of one and half kilo meters from here."

Ashok said "Dad, you both live here as we will be visiting you frequently. My family and Bala's family would be coming here for festivals and other functions. You can use a car for moving around."

Mohan seconded him "Yes, uncle, as the building is ready you can comfortably live here. That old house, could be let out if you want.'

Ashok and Mala in unison "Yes, Dad, you live here."

Mr. Krishnarao laughed and said "we will think over."

Mohan "The alternative choice of letting out is not good. One thing is the rates you get here are not good. Secondly, the building would be spoiled by the tenants, no doubt about that."

Ramya smiled and said "Uncle, my opinion is you should use both. Keep this building too furnished and whenever Ashok's or Bala's families visit, you can happily spend time here. If you feel contacts of the old town you miss, you can stay in the old house for some time. For functions too you need this. If you let it out it would be spoiled."

Mohan smiled and said "That's right. What Ramya spoke is right."

Mala too agreed with this solution.

Bala and Venkat liked the solution.

Mala said "Yes, father-in-law, you use both the houses. There is no necessity of rent, which is small any way. You must agree to use a car now."

She laughed, as her father-in-law sent back the car given by Ashok earlier, she referred to that.

Ashok too concurred "Yes Dad, you will have a car to move around, then you won't feel lonely. You please agree to this plan."

At last, Mr. Krishnarao accepted to the proposal and laughed happily for the attention shown for him by his family members and friends.

At that point of time, Babu, son of Ashok and Sree, daughter of Mohan came there, and with great joy shouted loudly to their mothers.

"Mom, this place is good, we will stay here for tomorrow too. We can play here freely."

Jaggu was smiling for their enthusiasm. He was older to them by a few years.

Ramya "Yes, you play well here without going to school, I know."

All of them laughed for the joke.

Ramya asked them "You played with whom?"

They said in one voice "With the watchman, he is good."

They laughed again.

* * *

30

Kashyap was able to get the machinery supplied and assembled at a place far away from Delhi. He did not mind travelling to a distant place, where the production was to start. His father-in-law lived in a remote village Narayanpur at a distance of hundred kilometers from Bareilly. No buses ply to that place, but power supply was there. Kashyap needed power supply and a remote place. So Narayanpur suited him.

He made a few sheds for the factory and some more sheds for the residence of workers. The sheds were well equipped, however.

The chemicals required in the padding of wooden planks were available at Pune and Mumbai. He contacted for regular supply of the materials. Each of the three chemicals were supplied by different dealers, two of them from Pune. The third was from Mumbai. He never disclosed the purpose for which he needed them. It appeared they did not know that those chemicals were used in making panels for replacing cement and bricks in construction activity.

Next important point was recruitment of personnel. He needed a foreman who was a reliable man. His own automobile parts company, had experienced workmen. Some of them were qualified and experienced too. One Shambudas was a reliable person and well versed in machinery parts making. He could work independently on earlier occasions. He had been working with him since more than a decade. He asked him if he was willing to work at a place like Narayanpur far from Delhi. With utmost persuasion, on offer of special bonuses for each year, he accepted to go there and work, as a foreman.

Some local youth were picked up and appointed as workmen. They were trained in the work by the foreman.

Ramesh was fixed there as manager and was offered a very attractive payment. He was promised to be designated as Deputy Director later.

After a month, the trial production was done. After some failures, the product became acceptable by the quality control machine.

After a fortnight they began regular production.

Next step was acceptance by the customer users.

Kashyap's father-in-law was making a new house at his place. With utmost persuasion he accepted to use the panels for the upstairs rooms. That was after Kashyap's offer of the panels free of cost.

The construction of the building was completed and it gave very good looks, particularly the upstairs rooms had a very neat finishing and time was also saved for finishing. The distemper colours gave a very beautiful appearance to the walls. The visitors who viewed the structure enquired about the good finish of the upstairs portion of the building. On the advice of Kashyap, his father-in-law told the visitors that the work of wood panels was the brain child of his son in law. He also told them that such wood panels were being used in foreign countries already.

Soon some users for house construction, enquired about the wood panels and got it procured from Kashyap, in his words. He said it was available at a faraway place and he could get them at high transport cost.

After three months, the Permanent Wood panels, became acceptable for their durability as two seasons had lapsed after the construction of his father-in-law's building. The wood panels stayed put through the rainy and summer seasons.

Kashyap's father-in-law was satisfied with the panels and started recommending them to his friends and acquaintances. The cost reduction was additional advantage. The finishing was good too. Time saved was beneficial to the contractors.

Kashyap became ambitious and he began supplying to small companies of big towns around Narayanpur.

Orders began coming from Lucknow city suburbs. He used discretion in supplying the panels and chose small construction companies and householders, selectively. He refused risky orders from big companies on the pretext that supply was limited or exhausted.

* * *

Venkat became suspicious when he came across such panelled walls at Delhi. The panels were of sizes and quality of wood different from their company. The finishing was inferior to their product.

He came to Delhi, on the invitation by his ex-colleague of Mumbai company, for his house warming ceremony at Vasant Vihar colony. He enquired about the novelty of the walls. His friend told him that his brother who worked at Lucknow got the wood panels supplied, which were used in the making of the walls. He said that in addition to the good finish, the cost of construction also reduced due to those wood panels. But he could not give the address of the supplier. He told Venkat that he would find out from his brother later and tell him, if he wants that. Venkat said he was interested in that as he wants to make a house at Vizag.

* * *

After returning to Vizag, Venkat told Ashok about the usage of the wood panels at Delhi. They checked the records and there was no supply to any Lucknow dealer. Ashok said the panels could have been supplied by Kashyap or any other dealer of Delhi.

Venkat said "But the type of wood panels used there is evoking suspicion."

He continued "Moreover our dealers supply to large sized consumers like construction companies only. This has not become popular with individual householders."

Ashok "We will check with Kashyap later. If any duplicate emerged, the dealers too are affected and hence, they will be alerted and we will get information at once."

Venkat "O.K., we will wait for any information from my friend and then talk to Kashyap or other dealers at Delhi."

Ashok "Yes, we should not create panic in dealers at Delhi for no reason. O.K., brother-in-law."

* * *

Venkat did not get any information from his friend at Delhi even after many weeks. The issue was forgotten.

* * *

After a month, Ashok got a phone call from Venkat.

"Ashok, I got a call from one dealer of Delhi, Moghul Wood Suppliers. They said that they came know some householders and Housing Societies were getting Power wood panels from some other sources."

Ashok asked "Did he complain to the President of the Dealers Association, Mr. Kashyap?"

Venkat "He said he casually told Kashyap about this. But Kashyap was not evincing any interest in the matter. So, he called me."

Ashok said "We will talk to Kashyap. You can call him, sir and find if anything is amiss."

Venkat agreed to that.

He called Kashyap and enquired about the supply of duplicate panels to a Housing Society. He expressed his ignorance. And he said that it could be some imported material."

On knowing the explanation of Kashyap, Ashok said "We must enquire with the Industries Department. We may not be able to get information from Imports and Exports Department. We can find out if any imports of such wood panels are allowed."

Venkat "I think, we can check in the booklet on Imports of the department for this information."

Ashok said "O.K., brother-in-law."

* * *

Ashok talked to Mohan about the suspected duplicate panels used at Delhi.

Mohan said "if there are no imports here what does that mean? Some other person or company is making the duplicate panels."

Ashok "That's what my brother-in-law said. He checked through the latest booklet on imports and did not contain any such item there."

Mohan "We must also inform the patent holder, the Research organisation about this breach of their patent."

He continued "We have to check with them, if they had given permission to any north Indian source for the production"

Ashok said "I will call them now and find out."

He called the Central Research organization for construction materials.

"Sir, I am Ashok from the Premium Wood Private Limited, Vizag. I want to talk to the patents department."

He was connected to the Manager.

He said "Yes, Mr. Ashok, what can I do for you?"

Ashok said "Sir, we are having the lease of patent for the new wood production."

The manager said "I know, you are the present patent holder. So, what now?'

"Recently we came to know someone is supplying similar version of new wood panels to small users, housing company residents. We are supplying to dealers they in turn supply to big users like construction companies only. And we now found out from our dealers that they had not supplied to those small users. Sir, I want to know if you have extended the patent again to some north Indian company."

"No, how can we do that? It is a breach of contract. We never gave permission to anyone. Now that you made this disclosure, we will make a complaint to appropriate authorities and will revert to you later."

Ashok said "Thank you, sir."

Manager "It is our duty to pursue this matter."

Ashok kept off the phone.

Ashok "Mohan, we made our case. They have not done any change in patent leasing. Now we have to wait and see."

Mohan "Do you want me to check at Delhi?"

Ashok "Of course that Research organisation will take action. But it will take time and in our own interest we could do something, I think."

Mohan "I will ask someone in Delhi, from my father-in-law's office to enquire for the source of supply."

Ashok "Yes, you can ask him to note the user's name and address from our dealer who talked to us about this. He can go to the users and approach them as if he represents our company and offer to supply the panels at a lower rate."

He continued "That way, we can approach the users."

Mohan "O.K., Ashok, I will do that. Let us see."

Ashok "We must act from our side, so that we do not lose business because of this fraudulence."

* * *

A week later, Mohan called Ashok.

"Ashok, I got the information from Delhi. My contact person talked to the Dealer who complained about the duplicate panels. He gave the address of the householder who used those panels. He responded to my contact and told that he got the supply from an agent whom the builder knew. The builder was not open to give information about the person who supplied the duplicate panels. So, the details were not available to common man. They are doing business through some agents. It could be ascertained by authorities only."

Ashok "Did you contact Kashyap?"

"I talked to Kashyap on phone. He was not forthcoming. His answer was that he was not aware of any such thing and his business was going on as usual. He also told that it was our botheration to check frauds if any, but not his. He was not cooperating and was disinterested in this. He appeared as if he was not affected by this fraud.

Ashok "Then we will wait for the information from the research organization. Of course, that takes time."

Mohan "It will be by the government authorities and we know how authorities work."

Ashok "Yes, I know. There appears to be no other answer to this."

Mohan "I think we could concentrate on the business in South India. We must increase our efforts to get more orders from those sources."

Ashok "We will sit with Mr. Venkat, my brother-in-law and the manager of the first factory."

Mohan "Yes, Ashok, you please call for a meeting and we will meet and discuss methods to get more orders."

Ashok "We will have to call a board meeting after our discussions. We may involve them too so that all the members know the happenings in the industry."

Mohan said "Yes Ashok, that is right."

* * *

31

Mohan's father-in-law, Mr. Maruthirao was unwell. Ramya called Mala and told her about that. Ashok called Mohan and enquired about the health of his father-in-law.

Mohan told him "He had chest pain on the back side three days back. He went to his family doctor. His B.P. was normal. He had been taking medicine for his chronic B.P. since many years. He was given some pain killer. He had some stomach problem too. That was bloating of stomach. His physician gave medicine for that too."

Ashok asked him "Is he stable now?"

Mohan "Yes, he is better now and taking rest as advised by the doctor. He is not attending to work now."

Ashok "Is he available at home?"

Mohan "Yes".

Ashok "I would like to see him."

Mohan "It's alright. You can visit him."

* * *

Ashok and Mala went to the house of Mr. Maruthirao, in New Journalist colony.

It's a posh locality. All bungalows were with high walls and security. It's only by name it's called Journalists' colony, but most of the buildings were owned by politicians or big business persons.

The watchman led them in. Ramya came out and took them to the upstairs bedroom, where her father was resting.

Ramya's father Maruthirao was lying on the bed next to a large window with curtains. He opened his eyes and smiled on seeing Mala and Ashok.

Mala asked him "How are you uncle?"

He replied "I am fine now, Mala."

He became weak in voice, but otherwise, he appeared healthy.

The maid pulled armless chairs near the bed for them to sit.

He said "I had bloated stomach with which I had been suffering often since many years. I took some homeo medicines as usual. But it did not subside. In the night, I had back pain. Our family doctor came and checked me. He said it was o.k. with me and nothing to worry."

Ramya's mother came and stood beside the bed keeping her arm on the chair of Ramya.

Maruthirao continued "the medicines worked alright and I had good sleep in the night. But doctor advised me rest for three days."

He smiled and thanked Mala and Ashok for visiting him.

Ramya's mother said "The doctor said he needed rest. I think he over-worked and that affected his health. He ate at a dinner party with the fellow members of the club. I think that gave the bloating problem."

Maruthirao smiled and said "That is common. Going to club and parties, you cannot avoid in the society."

Ashok "Uncle you please take rest. We should not disturb you."

He got up from his chair. Others too followed suit.

Mala and Ashok greeted him with folded hands. Maruthirao smiled and reciprocated without getting up from the bed.

Ramya led them to groundfloor hall. They sat there for some time. The maid brought them coffees.

After coffee Mala and Ashok left for home.

* * *

A week after that, Ashok received a call from Mohan. He was sad.

He said with a solemn voice "Ashok, my father-in-law expired this morning. The doctor's diagnosis was not correct. He had a heart attack the previous night. Please convey to Mala too."

Ashok expressed his condolences.

An hour later, Ashok and Mala went to Ramya's house to console her and her mother.

* * *

Mohan had a tough time, to cope up with the work at office with the absence of his father-in-law and Ramya's inability to work. The business affairs were to be continued. But Ramya in whose name her father wrote the will was not yet ready to take over. She could not recover from the grief of her father's death.

Mohan had to call the lawyer to attend to the formalities to make way for Ramya to take over companies, a Pharma company and a Jewellery export company her name was there as heir, but name of the third one, a Hard company was not mentioned in the will. The court had to be approached to declare Ramya as the successor if her mother forfeits her claim.

The head offices of the first two companies were at Vizag only. But the third one was registered as a company with head office at Delhi.

The company's lawyer filed a petition with the affidavits in the city civil court. He told Mohan that it would take at least two weeks to get the orders from the court.

* * *

After a week, Mohan got a call from the lawyer. He said the proceedings were stalled in the court as they received a claim from another party from Delhi, on the company at Delhi.

Mohan asked "Are there liabilities on the company sir?"

Lawyer "No, sir, it was a family matter. A person by name Sudhakar claims that he is a son of Maruthirao from his second wife, Jhansi."

Mohan was shocked. He said "We never knew any such thing."

Lawyer said "We have to pursue the matter in court. The claimant will be asked to be present in court, later. O.K. sir, we will take up the matter."

Mohan "We want to meet you, sir."

Lawyer "Yes, Mr. Mohan, you please bring Mrs. Ramya also with you."

* * *

Sudhakar, the claimant in the Delhi company episode, attended the court with his mother, Jhansi. He appeared bold and confident of his claim. He was in early thirties. His mother Jhansi was on the other side of fifties, but appeared younger and purposeful in her pursuit for the share of the properties. The tragedy of the death of her husband, Maruthirao, showed a shadow of sorrow on her face.

Their lawyer produced a series of photos of the mother and son with the deceased Maruthirao in happier days. He submitted to the court a copy of the will made by Maruthirao in respect of the Delhi company, favouring his second wife. It appeared the relationship was a long standing one at least more than the age of her son, Sudhakar.

Ramya's lawyer, representing his clients, Ramya and Mohan, pleaded for D.N.A. test. The court agreed though reluctantly. The preliminary evidence of photos and will in addition to umpteen letters written by Maruthirao had sufficiently proved their claim. But on the pleadings of the lawyer of Ramya and to clinch the evidence, the court agreed for the D.N.A. test. The court was adjourned for a month.

* * *

Ramya's mother felt embarrassed about the court proceedings of the relationship of her husband with a lady at Delhi.

Ramya and Mohan were surprised at the way Maruthirao could camouflage the affair for a few decades without giving any trace of doubt to them. The way the mother and son from Delhi, came to claim their right without embarrassment showed their confidence and rightfulness of the action on their part.

In their minds, Ramya and Mohan already came to the logical conclusion, based on the will, photos and documents produced by Sudhakar and his mother. The duo appeared to be from a dignified family, the way they kept their profile low. Ramya recognised the signature of her father on the will produced by them in the court.

* * *

In the meantime, Mohan and Ramya could get the required court orders for Ramya to take over the control of the two Vizag based companies. The work was resumed by Ramya without any hiccups.

* * *

32

Mohan could spend extra time on the work of Perfect Wood Production, as the Delhi based company of Ramya was lost to the other party in the court. The work of the two Vizag based companies of Ramya were well established with staff and they need not attend to them regularly. He called Ashok and said,

"Ashok, now that Ramya had to shed the management of the Delhi based company, I am feeling free to that extent and thought I must lessen your work at the Power wood companies."

Ashok" O.K., Mohan, thank you. Mrs. Jaya's husband, Bhaskar is yet to pick up work at office. Till that time, probably, you will be of help to upkeep the management of that company."

Mohan "I thought so."

Ashok "Did the court pass orders in the case of Delhi company?"

Mohan "Not yet. But they produced the D.N.A certificate. Our lawyer says that is authentic and proved the petitioner's contention. So, it is only question of days, we lose that company to the claimants."

He continued "Ashok, did the Research Organisation send any message?"

Ashok "Nothing. We will write a reminder to them."

Mohan "In the meantime we have to concentrate on South India demand. Shall we call the Board meeting?"

Ashok "Yes, I will talk to Rajesh."

Mohan "Regarding the Research Organisation, it might be better if we personally take up the matter with them. Do you want me to go there and meet the Director to request for early action?"

Ashok thought over and said "Of course, nothing like personal touch, if you find time."

He smiled appreciatively for the initiative shown by Mohan.

* * *

After four days, Mohan called Ashok and told him about his meeting with the Director of the Central Research Organisation [C.R.O.].

Ashok "Yes, Mohan, what is the news?"

Mohan "Ashok, I went to C.R.O. at Mumbai. The director explained things thread bare. He said it would take time to explore the fraud. The case was handed over to C.I.D of the U.P. state. As it was not a 'public interest litigation', in their words it was only a criminal act of fraud, the police give least importance. That is because, C.I.D has many local issues and they would be forced to give priority to the issues raised by the politicians. During the conversation, the director told me that one Kashyap, a dealer at Delhi visited them seeking a license in the sense lease of the patent for the North India trade. The director informed him that there is a lease in force on All India basis and his request was turned down. "

Ashok "Now I have a doubt why Ramesh left us and I think he must have joined Kashyap."

Mohan smiled and said "Yes, I also believe that Kashyap must be doing some work on the panel making at Delhi or some other place."

Ashok "Yes, Ramesh must have passed on the information about the process, machinery and so on to him."

Mohan smiled "Yes, the mystery is now solved. But we cannot do anything on our own. It is with the police there and we cannot do anything other than waiting."

Ashok "With the local police and political influence, Kashyap must have arranged everything and get going with the production of panels, usage of which Mr. Venkat came across at Delhi."

Mohan smiled "Our curiosity is answered now. Nothing more than that. We now better proceed with our earlier plan of concentrating on South India demand."

Ashok "I had asked Rajesh and he must be arranging the board meeting shortly."

* * *

The board meeting of Premium Wood Company Ltd. was attended by majority of the members except for Ramesh and Mr. Dasaradh.

Rajesh conducted the meeting as secretary.

Mohan as M.D. welcomed the members and said "Friends, we called the meeting to discuss mainly the matter pertaining to the fraud committed against our company by some unknown person making similar to our panels of wood in North India. We only came to know that similar wood panels are being made and sold at Delhi. They are being sold to individual householders and members of Housing societies. They are not selling to construction companies, perhaps not willing to go full speed, out of fear. Even that is a bad gesture putting us to loss of business. We made a complaint to the original patent holder, C.R.O and they had initiated action. The case is being dealt with by C.I.D. of the state of U.P. We are informed that it would take time to bring things to light.

So, in the meantime, we felt that we should increase the sales in the Southern India. We must exploit the novelty of the panels' usage and their effectiveness till we hold the lease.

Moreover, we don't know how things might change from time to time.

Such frauds happen in any business and duplicate products appear perennially.

So, we now propose to undertake more aggressive advertisement and reach out to more construction companies to get maximum demand for our original products.

"We call and invite you for discussion."

He sat down.

Dr. Varada stood up and asked "I agree with your proposal. But if duplicate panels are being made, don't we have any other way of stalling them? I mean to find out by our means the source of such makers and proceed legally against them. I know C.I.D. of state governments could be influenced and the fraud may not see the light of the day."

Mohan "What you said is hypothetically o.k., Dr. Varada, but who will do that job for us? We know that private detectives would do such jobs. But are they available and reachable for us now, I don't know?"

Sagar got up and said "Yes, we must pursue the matter. Otherwise, some other person may start production of panels near home even, if not in South India."

Mohan "Yes, Mr. Sagar, we will try to find out, about private agency who could do that for us."

Ashok got up and said "If we could lay our hands on the fraudster, we could file criminal case against them."

Then, Mohan said "We have to inform you about the resignation of Ramesh, our manager in factory one. We understand that he left this place and reached Delhi. He is one of the members here. He did not respond to our call for attending the Board meeting.

With this the topics for discussion are over. If anyone wants to bring any point for discussion, you may do that."

As there was no response, Ashok got up and thanked the members who attended the meeting.

The board meeting came to a close.

* * *

Mr. Kashyap was in his office at R.K. Puram, Delhi. He called for a meeting of dealers of wooden panels and other wood products. He wanted to know the demand for the wooden panels in different parts of the country, so that he could plan production in his factory. He could sell surreptitiously his illegal products till he could get a license for North India. Even after wards as a licensed producer he should be aware of the demands in the country. He did not want to restrict his sales to North India only, as there could not be a ban for his products in Sothern parts though produced in North India.

The meeting was planned to be held at the conference hall of All India Business Council, same day in the evening.

He called Ramesh to his office. Ramesh came to Delhi on his personal work with permission to leave Narayanpur for one day as next day was Sunday, being a holiday. His presence was required at the factory on all working days. Ramesh became busy with production picking up, as the orders for supply poured forth.

Ramesh asked Kashyap "Sir, do you want me attend the meeting in the evening?"

Kashyap laughed loudly "It's like keeping stolen goods in the open market. Never even come in to contact with those dealers, not until I get the license or lease whatever it is. I had talked to our M.P. Mr. Viswanath. He said it is not impossible to change the rules of the C.R.O. to provide for one more leaseholder in a different area. Those days, when Mr. Ashok got the lease, the efficacy of the wooden panels was not proved and hence the demand was less. Now, nobody can stop more manufacturers and more dealers. But he said, we have to spend a fortune to get things done."

Ramesh "My God, but at least, it is possible now. That's good news sir. How much we have to spend sir."

Kashyap laughed again and said "Yes, it is good news and I am very hopeful. You are lucky too. You may continue in the same factory which will become officially registered in course of time. Regarding the lease I will tap some other businessman or dealer who is good to me to join me. So, I need not spend the entire 'fortune' by myself. You understand?"

Ramesh "Yes, sir, I am lucky to come back to you."

Three months after that meeting, the C.R.O. had their rules amended to include a provision for giving lease state wise. Kashyap got the lease for U.P. along with another aspirant Mr. Ramnath. Ramesh became officially the manager of the Kashyap's factory at Rampur. Kashyap convinced Ramnath that they would open another factory near Delhi, in which both would be partners. Thus, Kashyap remained sole owner of the factory at Narayanpur.

* * *

33

Ashok came to know that Kashyap managed to get a licence for making special wood panels, for the state of U.P. The complaint, the C.I.D was trying to investigate was closed. The private detective agency to which the investigation was entrusted by Premium Wood Company Ltd. had to stop their work on that job, as it was no more illegal to make such wood panels in other areas. The payments made to that agency became a loss to the company now, with the changed rules.

But the happy ending was that the aggressive campaign made by the Premium Wood Company in South India yielded good results. They could increase the sales two-fold in three-month's time. The reason for that as told by Dr. Varada was that the power wood panels proved their worth in the market.

Mohan commented that they became the pioneers of special wood panels in India and helped the product to establish in the country. Of course, the advantage was reaped by all those who were in that business.

Mohan met Ashok in the office.

He said "Ashok, it is a reality now that production becomes more with more licences issued. We survive by diversifying additionally in to a different field of activity. Vertically one step down is Dealerships around India, one more step further down is to go for construction business."

Ashok laughed "Yes, what you told is correct, Mohan. In business it happens. But if not vertically down, we may also consider planning for horizontal expansion, like production of other construction materials in an inventive way."

Mohan "Yes, we must meet with Dr. Varada."

Ashok "Yes, I will call him for a meeting."

Mohan "You may also ask Mr. Venkat to be present."

Ashok "Yes, Mohan, we will do that."

* * *

Mohan, Ashok, Dr. Varada and Mr. Venkat met in the conference room of Premium Wood Products [P] Ltd.

Ashok said "Friends, we know we are outsmarted now in this business. Mr. Kashyap could now get a license for making the panels in North India. Of course, that happens in any business."

Mohan "Yes, that's right. But we have missed one important point. In business, monopoly would not last forever. We could have taken care to establish well by producing more and selling more."

Dr. Varada smiled and said "Not only that you could have started your own dealerships chain to the extent possible."

Venkat "Another drawback is the limitation of production facility."

Dr. Varada said "That's right. Even now we need not get disheartened. Instead of beating on quantity, we can out beat on grounds of quality and also price. Please concentrate on that."

Mohan "Dr. Varada, in fact we wanted to meet you on another aspect. Expansion on vertical level is difficult, of course quality and price are there to do that. We thought of horizontal expansion to circumvent the competition. What I mean we must think of venturing in to other areas of construction. We request you to advise us on that issue."

Dr. Varada "Of course, I will keep my sight on that aspect. But it will take time."

Ashok "Yes, Dr. Varada, as you suggested we will concentrate on aspects of quality and price."

Mohan "In quality, you please make some suggestions for improvement."

Venkat "Yes, there may be chances of improving the life of the panels. Another thing is instead of single size, multiple sizes could be explored."

Mohan "Yes, please suggest any method of doing that. Is it necessary to modify the machinery for that?"

Dr. Varada "Yes, I will consider that too."

The meeting then concluded with a visit to the factory site, to have a look at the production cycle, on the desire of Dr. Varada.

* * *

After a month of the meeting, Dr. Varada called Ashok and met him in his office. He explained all the aspects he was asked to explore in the meeting. He said,

"Mr. Ashok, regarding the quality of the panels, you must make sure that you use the same quality and check the efficacy of the materials. For that, materials of I.S.I. standard are to be used. Then more important is the brand image. We have to get Indian Standards Institute [I.S.I.] certification, so that we can print I.S.I. emblem on each finished panel. I checked with them and they have not given any standard for the wooden panels yet. We have to write to them to fix standards for the panels. We must send our samples when they ask, period wise and may be cycle wise too, to them."

Ashok "We will write to them. You please help us in drafting a suitable letter. How long it will take for the standard to emerge, we don't know."

Dr. Varada "I cannot say. It depends on the time required for fixing the standard and also their present schedule. We will have to pursue the matter suitably. We may have to meet the concerned officials."

Ashok "Yes, Dr. Varada. We will do that. About wood planks, I will talk to Mohan, to check for good quality planks from time to time and Mr. Venkat too. I will inform them about our discussion and also about the materials."

Dr. Varada "By acquiring the I.S.I. standard we stand better chance, to market our goods."

Ashok "Dr. Varada, we must also think of the choice of sizes of planks. We can have an edge, if we have varied standard sizes as required by the construction companies. The problem now is, we cannot cut the finished panel, as the edges lose their coating of chemicals and would be exposed to atmospheric damage."

Dr. Varada "Yes, I thought over, about that. The standard sizes of usage cannot be more than five or so. Length wise, we have ceilings of heights eight, nine or ten feet. About horizontal lengths, we must find out the number of sizes, generally, the construction companies need."

Ashok "But, can our machines provide for each type of finished product?"

"No, we must have suitable frames to keep the wooden planks in position and the machine must have instrumentation to choose them. You have to check with the machine makers about that. But it must be very costly to get them and may be, they will not be available at once. It would take time and plenty of money."

He continued "Alternatively we must have cutting machines to cut the finished planks to sizes required and then the chemicals can be applied to the edges either by machines or even manually to cut the cost."

Ashok smiled and said "The second would be suitable to our financial position and also to get things done fast."

Dr. Varada "O.K. Mr. Ashok, please think over. Regarding standards, I will draft a letter to I.S.I. and send it to you."

Ashok "Thank you. Dr. Varada."

* * *

Premium Wood Company [P] Ltd, wrote a letter to the I.S.I, New Delhi.

After a week to that, Ashok and Mohan discussed and decided that one of them must visit that office personally to get things move fast. Mohan offered to go and talk to them personally and also to find out ways to move the matter fast, as it happens in government offices.

Mohan went to Delhi and met the Director at the I.S.I. office.

Director said "Mr. Mohan, how long you have been in this business?"

Mohan "Since, six years, sir."

"Your application for fixing the standards is O.K. The C.S.O. being semi-government organization, the process and product need not further be assessed. We have to check the panels made by you from time to time and see whether they confirm to the standard of the I.S.I. It will take time."

Mohan "Are we to pay fees, sir."

Director "Of course, you pay fees at the office counter. Are you sure your panels could be used by common man safely? I mean middle class householders. It is very important, because, he cannot afford to lose on quality while planning to save money on using your panels."

Mohan "Certainly, sir. My partner Ashok, used these panels for making his own house. That was four years back. It is quite fine now."

Director "I am making a house at Hyderabad. You mean to say, I can use them safely there?"

Mohan "Certainly sir. We will send sample planks sir, when you happen to be there."

"O.K., next month first two weeks I will be there."

"O.K. sir, I will send the samples there, after finding out your availability there."

He continued after a pause "Sir, how long it will take to get I.S.I standard?'

"May be three months or even more, it depends. You please pursue the matter with the office. You can contact one, Mr. Chatterjee in the office."

Mohan "Thank you, sir. I will call you next month and send a person with the samples."

The Director gave him his visiting card and said "O.K. Mr. Mohan."

* * *

Mohan called Ashok when he was free from his work, and met him in his office. It was more than a week since they met last. He had to discuss the details he talked with the Director at the office of I.S.I.

Mohan said "Yes, Ashok, that appears to be a positive response. As you said some time back personal touch helps in solving or pushing things to expeditious results."

Ashok smiled "I am glad things are moving fast and towards positive results. Did you pay the fees required for I.S.I. certification or it may be for establishing a standard?"

"Yes, I paid the fee by cheque. Next month, I promised to send samples of the planks to the Director's house under construction at Hyderabad. I have to call him then. I told I will send him a person with the samples."

Ashok smiled and said "O.K., we will send extra panels for his use. He expects that. That means, he had heard about the efficacy of the panels already."

Mohan smiled "I know. I thought the same way. How many panels we send?"

Ashok thought over and said "I think we can send for one floor of two thousand square feet. Mr. Venkat can assess that."

Mohan "Then, about the standard sizes. I mean extra sizes as required by users, what is the plan? "

"I told you as Mr. Varada said, we cut the finished panels to the required sizes, and apply the chemicals to the edges manually for now, till we get machinery for that work."

"Regarding the quality of wood planks, I have already told our men at Rajahmundry, to maintain the standard of the planks good and same always."

Ashok "So, we have solved the quality requirement and also demand for some sizes for now."

Mohan "We have done the spade work for the I.S.I. standard and expect the result in about three months. I will pursue with Mr. Chatterjee of that office as advised by the Director."

"With samples being sent to him, the I.S.I. work also would move fast. Next as discussed in the meeting is, price reduction."

"Yes, that is important, from the demand point of view. One is I.S.I. mark and the second is lower price."

"First we will find out the prices of our competitors."

Mohan "We will find out from our dealers. "

Ashok "Coming to the subject of dealers, we would also plan to have our own dealers at some cities in all states or as many as possible. We provide goods without taking advance and they have to arrange the commercial places."

"Mr. Venkat could do that. He is an experienced executive."

"With that we discussed all the points we were to attend to."

"We will have to pursue the matters of sizes, price and I.S.I."

Ashok "Yes, Mohan. You have come in time to finish the points of discussion. Thank you."

Mohan "O.K. we will meet again."

* * *

Mr. Venkat introduced in the process, the method of making a few standard sizes of panels with the process of cutting the larger panels in to smaller sizes and applying the chemicals to edges. He concentrated on effecting cost reduction methods in purchasing and usage of materials.

The ultimate effect of cost savings reflected in reduced prices of finished panels. The material sold by Premium Wood Company became very competitive and had out beaten other products in the market.

As told by the Director and with the cooperation of Mr. Chatterjee of I.S.I., the standards for power wood panels were released without much delay.

After submitting a few panels periodically for a few weeks, Premium Wood Company could get I.S.I. number and marking for their products.

* * *

34

Ashok's company Maxima Productions began losing its business. The orders received were less, during the latest year compared to the year before. Ashok got information that some central minister evinced interest in that business. A close relative of the minister was in the machine parts business. Political pressures were common in business dealings.

Ashok thought of the matter for some time. He did not come to any conclusion, either to continue, divert or close the company. After a week of indecision, he consulted Dr. Varada.

Dr. Varada said "Mr. Ashok, you asked me some time back about horizontal expansion in your Premium Wood Company. I had been on that job, but right now, I could not lay my hands on any specific solution. But with your new problem with this Maxima Production, I have one suggestion. Of course, there are two options, one is to close the company and put for sale and other to diversify the production line. When the second one is not possible you sell it. I thought of the diversification of the line of production. You are having machinery for making various machine parts. We know that your wood panel making requires machinery."

Ashok smiled and excused for interruption "But, I don't require so much machinery for making parts required for my wood panel company. "

Dr. Varada "I know. It is not for you alone. In course of time, many more establishments would spring up as the business of wood panels is such. It is a growing business. So, you can plan to make machinery and parts for wood panel companies existing and coming forth in future. You consider this for the present."

Ashok "I will think over. I am also thinking of converting this company in to a private limited company with Mohan and some more partners. So, I will also talk with Mohan."

Dr. Varada "Certainly, that's a good idea. I mean the idea of converting this in to a company. It would take care of financial burden. Better to adopt this, to even out, the risks too."

Ashok "Thank you, Dr. Varada."

* * *

Ashok called Mohan for a discussion.

They met in the conference room.

Ashok informed Mohan about the problems faced by Maxima Productions. He also told him about the suggestions made by Dr. Varada; that of diversifying the production for making machine parts for companies in special wood products.

Ashok said "Dr. Varada told that the diversification could be for machine parts or even machinery required for special wood making companies. If not, he said I could close and sell off the company. There is no better way of coming out of the issue."

Mohan "With so much experience in this business, you should not think of disposing of the company. We can explore the possibility of making machine parts to start with. We can also think of making frames to make different sizes of panels and instrumentation required for that."

Ashok "Yes, we will do that. We can take the help of my brother-in-law. He is an experienced engineer."

Mohan "Yes, Mr. Venkat will be very useful for this purpose."

Ashok "I am also thinking of converting Maxima in to a limited company and take some members. If you don't mind my suggestion, you are welcome to become one of the members in the company."

Mohan "Certainly, Ashok. When you are offering membership in a company like Maxima, I must thank you. Why should be you be hesitant in making a favour to me?"

Ashok laughed "Then it is O.K., you know I require funds to run that company after planning for diversification."

Mohan laughed "I know we had already faced such problems in Premium Wood Company."

Ashok "I was in fact worried about Maxima. Now I am confident, with your support."

Mohan laughed "We are together these many years and will continue now."

* * *

In course of time, the I.S.I. stamping started to give its impact on buyers' mind.

After a few weeks the implementation of supplying other sizes, instead of one standard size too had its own effect. The demand for the panels of Premium Wood products and Perfect wood products slowly picked up.

Mr. Venkat advertised for dealership applications from medium sized cities and other smaller towns on the condition that supply of special wood panels would be made without advance payments, if commercial spaces would be provided by the aspirant dealers.

Applications began coming forth. Based on the credit-worthiness, Venkat started to appoint regular dealers.

* * *

The reduced demand for his products and the advertisements for dealers by Premium Wood Company did not go unnoticed by Kashyap and made him shaky. Wood panel stocks in his go-downs began piling up. Due to lack of sufficient turnover in business, funds position weakened. As a consequence, production of panels was retarded.

As there was no regular production, Ramesh's presence at Narayanpur became unnecessary. Kashyap asked Ramesh to shift to his machine parts factory near Delhi. His allowances were reduced. Later, even the factory at Narayanpur was shut. The production at the newly started wood panels factory near Delhi, in partnership with Ramnadh continued.

* * *

Dinakar was in tea shop near the company, sipping tea, during the lunch break.

"Hi, Dinakar."

Dinakar looked up to see Ramesh sitting down, opposite him.

He said "Hi, Mr. Ramesh, how is it, you are here, unexpected."

Ramesh "Dinakar, I happened to visit my sister here. Her daughter's marriage is going to be celebrated tomorrow. How is the work going on, here?"

Dinakar "Fine. The sales have picked up. We are very busy now."

Ramesh "What about Perfect wood production? Who is the manager now?"

"Both are in full swing. Mr. Bhaskar is the manager now, after you left the company. What about you? How is the work there?"

Ramesh with a gloomy face, Said, "The demand for our products is reduced. Mr. Kashyap said we are going to close Narayanpur factory. I am now at Delhi in his old workshop."

"What products?"

Ramesh laughed "You don't know? Mr. Kashyap started same special wood factory at Narayanpur. I am talking of that."

"I am sorry. What are you planning now?"

"I don't know. For the present I am in his workshop. At Delhi cost of living is high. Added to that, I am not getting some allowances, what I used get at Narayanpur."

Dinakar finished his tea and left the place, after taking leave of Ramesh.

* * *

Ashok called Mohan and Rajesh for discussing about the Maxima products.

They assembled in the conference room.

Ashok began "Mr. Rajesh, the Maxima Products is not functioning well now, due to increase in competition. I want to diversify the production in to machine parts making for special wood panels manufacturing."

Rajesh "That's a good change over. Now that many more companies are coming up for producing those special wood panels."

Ashok "One more thing. I want to convert Maxima in to a Private Limited company. That is why we have assembled now. Please do the needful for that. Mohan is one of the members to start with."

Mohan "As you said, Ashok, I talked to Mr. Narender, my uncle, He agreed for his son Sagar to join Maxima."

Ashok "Mr. Venkat is also ready to join us. I already talked to him."

Mohan "So, in total now we are four members. Do you have anybody else in mind?"

Ashok "I only have to ask Mr. Rajesh now?"

Rajesh "I will think over. It depends on the amount of investment needed. But I don't mind joining with small amount or small number of shares."

Ashok "O.K., Mr. Rajesh, you are in, with whatever you are ready to invest."

Mohan "How about Dr. Varada, our consultant?"

Ashok "He declined. He is not ready."

Rajesh "So, with these five members, including me, I will prepare papers and file the application."

Ashok "O.K., Mr. Rajesh."

They had coffees, brought by the office boy. Mr. Rajesh left.

Mohan asked "Why is Mr. Venkat not in this discussion?"

Ashok "He said he is busy with some urgent work."

Mohan "Any way, I will ask him to come, because we have to ask him about the changes in machine set up for making machinery parts at Maxima."

Ashok "Yes, Mohan, that is necessary. Otherwise, the labour and machinery would be lying idle as there is not sufficient work now."

Ashok called Mr. Venkat on intercom. Venkat said he would come for half hour time and arrived there in ten minutes.

Venkat said "Hi Mohan. Now we are going to become busy with Maxima again."

Ashok said "Brother-in-law, as I told you we are going to make machine parts for wood panel making machines at Maxima. In that connection we have to find out what kind of changes are to be made in machinery setup there. Mr. Rajesh discussed about the conversion of the firm in to a company. We have included you and Mr. Rajesh in addition to Sagar, as members."

Venkat "O.K., regarding the machinery set up there, we have to visit Maxima one day and check-up."

Ashok "The earlier the better, when will we go there? You please tell me."

Venkat "Tomorrow, forenoon I can spend with you."

Ashok "So, Mohan, we are going there tomorrow morning?"

Mohan "Yes, I will be here by eight in the morning, tomorrow."

Venkat said "O.K., we will meet here tomorrow."

* * *

35

Rajesh completed all the formalities for converting the firm, Maxima products as M/S Maxima products [P] Ltd.

Later, after choosing a day convenient to all the prospective members, he called for a meeting of the company. The five members attended the meeting.

Ashok was made Managing Director. Mohan refused to be a director as he was busy with the companies of Ramya in addition to his involvement in special wood companies. After consulting Narender, they made him the Chairman. Thus, Mr. Narender was also made a member and director. An amount of thirty lakhs of new investment plus the existing value of assets made the paid-up capital equivalent to fifty lakhs. Authorised capital was fixed at one crore, keeping in view the expansion required to take care of rising demand for machinery parts.

It was the first meeting of the new company. The process of election of M.D and the Chairman were formalized.

After completing the meeting of Maxima Products Ltd., Ashok addressed the members connected with all the three units to bring forth the details of things happened since last meeting.

He said "Dear members, now we have consolidated our efforts to form three production units, two companies and a firm. Premium Wood Products Pvt. Ltd. and Perfect Wood Products are for production of special wood panels and the third one Maxima Products Pvt. Ltd. is for making machinery parts required for the first two units and also meeting the demand for machinery parts of other special wood making companies in the country. The machine parts making activity will start shortly and we have the facility ready by upgrading the setup at Maxima to suit this purpose. With the cooperation of all the members, we are able make these units run smoothly.

I.S.I. standards are implemented in wood panels making. Next as per the demand of consumers, we are supplying required sized panels in our units. Because of these improvements, our products have become very competitive in the market.

Lastly, we have to now implement, the process of lowering the prices, wherever possible. That aspect Mr. Rajesh will take care of.

I thank you all for following the activity through thick and thin for success of our endeavours.

The meeting was closed with that.

* * *

Venkat reminded Ashok to discuss the cost reduction process and price control with Rajesh.

Ashok called a meeting with Mohan and Rajesh at the conference room. Mr. Venkat was there too.

Ashok asked Rajesh "Mr. Rajesh, we wanted to discuss about price reduction of our products. All other aspects were resolved, I think. Mohan and Mr. Venkat have to express their opinions."

Mohan said "At present, our products have an edge over others in the market. I had learnt recently that Dinakar of our company met Ramesh, our ex-manager and it appears that he confirmed our assessment that we are now better in market than other production units. Kashyap, had stopped production of wood panels and also shifted Ramesh from his factory. That proves our conviction, in the sense, our efforts on quality, standards, and supply of panels of different sizes have succeeded. Regarding the funds position, Mr. Venkat I suppose may like to speak about dealers and recoveries."

Venkat said "Recoveries from the dealers is a continuous process. Some are habitually regular. Regarding others, we have regulated the supplies according to payment. That is to be controlled. The only other aspect is payment to suppliers of materials by us. We have to watch the matching of the two, receipts from dealers and payments to suppliers, to reduce overdrafts with bankers and as on date we are fine."

Rajesh said "Yes, Mr. Ashok, regarding the price reduction, we have to effect cost reduction. Materials and labour costs, we cannot have much say, as the quality decides their utility value. Materials part we have standardised receipts of supplies. As this a process unit, labour activity is predetermined. The cost of production includes materials, labour and fixed costs. We have to add up financial costs like interest. The maximum price will be material plus labour plus fixed cost like depreciation plus finance cost and we add standard profit element to that. We fix price, keeping a comparison with market price. If we want to find our minimum cost, we can only reduce some percentage of fixed cost. Fixed cost like depreciation on machinery and buildings had already been incurred. So, we could recover some reduced value during the time of heavy competition or actual cost at other times. We will have to keep in view, the total to be recovered over the years, that is during the lifetime of the asset. That means we have to review the material cost and finance cost. Labour cost can be controlled by optimizing productivity. We can have review meetings every month."

Mohan smiled and said "You have explained business matters in a clear way, without high sounding terminology. Thank you, Mr. Rajesh. We will have review meetings as fixed by Mr. Ashok."

Venkat "Yes, that's a good proposal."

Ashok "Mr. Rajesh, you please prepare the price control chart and I think those have to be revised periodically depending on prices of materials and so on. You please decide on the monthly meetings in consultation with Mr. Venkat. We will follow them."

Mohan "With that many of the issues to be considered, have been discussed. So, Ashok, anything else?"

Ashok "That's all. Thank you, Mr. Rajesh and all. We will meet whenever Mr. Venkat and Mr. Rajesh call next."

* * *

Epilogue

After two weeks they have upgraded the machinery setup at Maxima, to produce machinery parts for special wood panel making machinery.

Mr. Venkat had set in motion, sending the information of availability of machine parts to special wood panels making companies.

There were enquiries for supply of entire machinery for such special wood panel making. Mr. Venkat informed them that he would be ready for supply of such machinery after a month, so as not to give a negative reply, as the business ethics say.

* * *

The activity of business was going on. The families of the entrepreneurs grew by years.

Ashok proved that his method of give and take, in all conditions of daily life, succeeds.

* * *